ACE Certified Personal T Exam Prep

A concise study guide that highlights the key concepts required to pass the American Council on Exercise (ACE) CPT Exam to become a certified personal trainer.

* Includes the "Key Concepts" that contain information needed for the exam.

* Includes quick reference pages for required Formulas, Conversions & Acronyms.

* Includes 50 practice questions to further enhance knowledge & to have an idea of what actual test will look like.

* Includes detailed practice question answers with explanations on how the answers were obtained.

* Includes detailed descriptions of assessments, the heart, muscles, nutrition, term definitions, training modalities and more.

For additional insights or to leave feedback visit our Facebook page below.
https://www.facebook.com/CPTPrep

Your feedback is welcomed and appreciated!

Copyright © 2016 by CPT Exam Prep

All rights reserved. No part of this publication may be reproduced, distributed, or transmitted in any form or by any means, including photocopying, recording, or other electronic or mechanical methods, without the prior written permission of the publisher, except in the case of brief quotations embodied in critical reviews and certain other noncommercial uses permitted by copyright law.

This book is intended to supplement, not replace the information provided in *American Council on Exercise Personal Trainer Manual (Fifth Edition)*.

Table of Contents

ACE Certified Personal Trainer Performance Domains 1
ACE Certified Personal Trainer Test Statistics 1

Domain I: Initial Client Interviews & Assessments 2
Client Consultation Forms 2
Risk Stratification 2
Signs or symptoms of cardiovascular, pulmonary or metabolic disease (CVD) 2
Risk Factors 3
Absolute & Relative Contraindications 4
Physiological & Psychological benefits of regular exercise 5
Sequence of Assessments 6
Heart Rate & Body Composition Assessments 7
Skill, Muscular & Cardiorespiratory Fitness Considerations 8
Posture & Movement Term Definitions 9
Static Posture Assessments 9
Movement Observations & Assessments 10
Skeleton & Spine, Types of Joints 11
Planes of Motion, Types of Movements & Location Term Definitions 12
Movement Term Definitions 13
The Heart 13
Heart Rate & Blood Pressure 14
Stroke Volume & Cardiac Output 15
Muscles 16
Muscle Action & Term Definitions 17

Domain II: Program Design & Implementation 18
Common Resistance-Training Myths & Mistakes 18
Training Principles 18

Table of Contents

Term Definitions & Types of Training Programs 19

Training Considerations 20

Detraining, Rhabdomyolysis, Valsalva maneuver & One Rep Max (1RM) test 21

Training Volume Based on Goals 22

Methods of Estimating Exercise Intensity 23

Energy Systems & Energy Pathways 24

ACE Integrated Fitness Training Model (ACE IFT) 25

Functional Movement & Resistance Training 26

Phase 1: Stability & Mobility Training, Phase 2: Movement Training 26

Phase 3: Load Training 27

Phase 4: Performance Training 28

Cardiorespiratory Training (Phases 1 – 4) 29

Mind-Body Exercise 30

Stretching Techniques 31

Movements of major muscle groups (Biomechanics) & Spotting Techniques 32

Nutrition & Human Performance 33

Fluid & Hydration, Nutrition & Health 34

Nutrition Scope of Practice & The Female Athlete Triad 35

Domain III: Program Progression & Modifications 36

The Transtheoretical Model (TTM) 36

The Health Belief model (HBM), Behavior-Change Strategies 37

Client-Trainer Relationship 38

Communication & Teaching Techniques 39

Types of Learners, Types of Feedback, & Client Feedback 40

Adherence to Exercise & Overcoming Barriers 41

Special Populations Exercise Recommendations 42

Table of Contents

Domain IV: Professional Conduct, Safety, & Risk Management 46

    ACE Certified Personal Trainer Scope of Practice 46

    Business Plan 46

    Six Basic Business Models 47

    Legal Documentation & Laws 48

    Risk Management Program 49

    Emergency Procedures, Injury Prevention Program, & When to call 9-1-1 50

    Common Medical Emergencies & Injuries 51

    Musculoskeletal Injury Terms, Overuse Conditions & Upper-Extremity Injuries 53

    Lower-Extremity Injuries 54

    The Healing Process 55

Acronym & Abbreviation Meanings 56

Conversions & Formulas 59

Practice Questions 60

Practice Question Answers 71

Resources & Helpful Links 74

Thank You Page 75

References 76

ACE Certified Personal Trainer Performance Domains

Domains are listed below with percentage of questions out of the 150 multiple choice questions on test. You are scored on 125 out of the 150 questions on the test. A passing score is 500 or better out of a possible 800 points (roughly 6.4 points per question).

Domain I: Client Interviews & Assessments – 31% (39+/- Questions)
Domain II: Program Design & Implementation – 33% (41+/- Questions)
Domain III: Program Progression & Modifications – 19% (24+/- Questions)
Domain IV: Professional Conduct, Safety, & Risk Management – 17% (21+/- Questions)

ACE Certified Personal Trainer Test Statistics

2015: 13,103 candidates took the test with a pass rate of 65%
(8,517 passed / 4,586 failed)

2014: 12,012 candidates took the test with a pass rate of 67%
(8,048 passed / 3,964 failed)

2013: 10,452 candidates took the test with a pass rate of 67%
(7,003 passed / 3,449 failed)

There are currently 44,621 ACE Certified Personal Trainers as of December 31st 2015.

You can become one by making sure you are prepared come test day!

This study guide was written to help enhance the knowledge required to become an ACE Certified Personal Trainer (CPT) and to give you the confidence that you are prepared come test day. Once you become certified this guide can be used to reference important information as you begin your career as a personal trainer.

Domain I: Client Interviews & Assessments

Create a credible and trusting relationship with clients to obtain relevant health and lifestyle information necessary for successful program design and outcomes.

Client Consultation Forms

Below is a list of the necessary and recommended forms for the initial client consultation.

Informed consent *(assumption of risk)*
Liability waiver
Physical activity readiness questionnaire (PAR-Q)
Health-history questionnaire *(Medical history, medications & supplements, exercise history, illnesses or injuries, lifestyle information such as nutrition, stress, work, sleep, etc.)*
Exercise history and attitude questionnaire *(important for developing goals & designing programs)*
Medical release *(if necessary once risk stratification has been completed)*
Testing forms *(used to record testing & measurement data during the fitness assessment)*
Client-Personal trainer agreement *(Agreement to participate)*

Risk stratification is used to determine a client's risk level **(Low, Moderate, or High)** for exercise and the appropriate procedures to follow once the risk classification is known. The following information describes how to determine which category a client is in based on signs and symptoms suggestive of **Cardiovascular Disease (CVD)** and known **Risk Factors**.

Signs or symptoms of cardiovascular, pulmonary or metabolic disease

- Pain or discomfort in the chest, neck, jaw, arms, or other areas that may result from ischemia
- Shortness of breath at rest or with mild exertion
- Orthopnea or paroxysmal nocturnal dyspnea *(shortness of breath / coughing in sleep)*
- Ankle edema *(swollen ankles)*
- Palpitations or tachycardia *(unpleasant forceful or rapid beating of the heart)*
- Intermittent claudication *(pain in muscle with inadequate blood supply that is stressed by exercise)*
- Known heart murmur
- Unusual fatigue or shortness of breath with usual activities
- Dizziness or syncope *(loss of consciousness)*

***Note**: If a client has any known CV, pulmonary, metabolic disease or has any major signs & symptoms suggestive of those diseases then they are automatically put in the **High Risk** Category. High risk individuals should have a **medical examination** prior to exercise and doctor supervision of exercise test performed.*

Risk Factors

Know these risk factors inside & out. Pay attention to greater than or equal to numbers like fasting glucose. For example a man who is 45 with a fasting glucose of 100 would be considered to have 2 risk factors.

Age: Men ≥45 years old, Women ≥55 years old

Family History: Myocardial infarction (heart attack), coronary revascularization, or sudden death before 55 years old in father or other male first-degree relative or before 65 years old in mother or other female first degree relative.

Cigarette Smoking: Current cigarette smoker or those who quit within the previous 6 months, or exposure to environmental tobacco smoke (secondhand smoke)

Sedentary Lifestyle: Not participating in at least 30 minutes of moderate intensity physical activity (40% to <60% VO_2R) on at least 3 days of the week for at least 3 months.

Obesity: BMI (Body Mass Index) ≥30 or waist girth >102cm (40 inches) for men and >88 cm (35 inches) for women

Hypertension: Systolic blood pressure ≥140 mm Hg and/or diastolic ≥90 mm Hg, confirmed by measurements on at least two separate occasions, or currently on antihypertensive medication.

Dyslipidemia: Low-density lipoprotein cholesterol ≥130 mg or high-density lipoprotein cholesterol <40 mg or on lipid-lowering medication. If total serum cholesterol is all that is available, use ≥200 mg.

Prediabetes: Impaired fasting glucose = fasting plasma glucose ≥100 mg but ≤125 mg or impaired glucose tolerance = two-hour values in oral glucose test ≥140mg but ≤199 mg confirmed by measurements on at least two separate occasions.

Negative Risk Factor: High-density lipoprotein (HDL) cholesterol ≥60 mg *(if any other risk factors are present this nullifies or takes one away)*

\> Greater than
≥ Greater than or equal to
< Less than
≤ Less than or equal to

Once the client's risk factors are determined use the **Risk Classification Chart** *(Figure 6-3 on Page 121 of American Council on Exercise Personal Trainer Manual - Fifth Edition)* to determine the client's risk classification **(Low or Moderate)** and the appropriate steps to follow. Anything over 1 risk factor ≥2 puts them at Moderate risk & 1 or less risk factor puts them at Low risk.

Absolute Contraindications
The risks of exercise testing outweigh the potential benefit. Client should not participate in exercise testing until conditions are stabilized or treated.

- Significant change in resting ECG.
- Unstable angina (chest pain)
- Uncontrolled cardiac dysrhythmias
- Severe symptomatic aortic stenosis
- Uncontrolled symptomatic heart failure
- Acute pulmonary embolus or pulmonary infarction
- Acute myocarditis or pericarditis
- Suspected or known dissecting aneurysm
- Acute systemic infection, accompanied by fever, body aches, or swollen lymph glands

Relative Contraindications
The benefits of exercise outweigh the risk. Exercise testing can be done only after careful evaluation of the risk/benefit ratio.

- Left main coronary stenosis
- Moderate stenotic valvular heart disease
- Electrolyte abnormalities
- Severe arterial hypertension
- Tachydysrhythmia or bradydysrhythmia (fast or slow heart rate)
- Hypertrophic cardiomyopathy and other forms of outflow tract obstruction
- Neuromuscular, musculoskeletal or rheumatoid disorders that are exacerbated by exercise
- High-degree atrioventricular block
- Ventricular aneurysm
- Uncontrolled metabolic disease
- Chronic infectious disease
- Mental or Physical impairment leading to inability to exercise adequately.

Certain medications or drugs may affect a client's ability to perform or respond to exercise. *Table 6-2 on Page 133 of American Council on Exercise Personal Trainer Manual - Fifth Edition* describes the effects medications have on heart-rate response. Any client taking medication that could potentially have an effect on exercise should have a physician's clearance for physical activity.

Although regular physical activity increases the risk of musculoskeletal injury and cardiovascular problems, the overall physical activity risk in the general population is low, especially compared to the health benefits of regular exercise.

Physiological benefits of regular exercise

- Improvement in cardio & respiratory function
- Reduction in coronary artery disease risk factors
- Decreased morbidity & mortality
- Decreased risk of falls
- Increased metabolic rate
- Improvement in bone health
- Weight loss and reduced obesity

Psychological benefits of regular exercise

- Decreased anxiety & depression
- Enhanced feelings of well being
- Positive affect on stress
- Better cognitive function

Regular exercise is a key component of long-term weight management. The following is a list of benefits that exercise has in effective weight loss and maintaining a healthy weight:

1) Exercise enhances daily caloric expenditure
2) Exercise, especially strength training, can minimize the loss of lean body mass.
3) Exercise may suppress appetite and counteract the impact that diet may have on resting metabolic rate (RMR).
4) Exercise makes the body more efficient at burning fat.

Adults should engage in at least **150 minutes** of moderate-intensity or 75 minutes of vigorous-intensity aerobic physical activity or a combination of both each week to improve overall health & fitness. Additional health benefits are obtained from performing more than 150 minutes of activity each week which also helps to further assist & maintain weight loss.

Overweight & obese individuals seeking to manage their weight should perform at least **300 minutes** of moderate-intensity or 150 minutes of vigorous-intensity exercise or activity or a combination of both each week.

The daily amount of exercise can be performed in one continuous bout or broken up into smaller bouts of at least 10 minutes or more throughout the day.

Trainers should place the needs and abilities of their clients first & progress to the recommended weekly training durations only when suitable for the client, based on their conditioning level, tolerance & availability.

Sequence of Assessments

Initial needs assessments should begin with reviewing a client's health history, completing the intake forms and questionnaires, discussing desires, preferences, general goals and then determining which assessments are relevant and a timeline to conduct them. Periodic reassessments are important to gauge a client's progress towards goal achievement.

Sample assessment sequencing for the general client can be found in Figure 5-2 on Page 94 of American Council on Exercise Personal Trainer Manual - Fifth Edition.

1) **Health-risk appraisal**
2) **Resting vital signs**: Heart rate and blood pressure
3) **Body Composition**: Height, Weight, Body Mass Index (BMI), Waist to Hip Ratio (WHR), Skin fold measurements *Quarterly body composition assessments are appropriate.*
4) **Static posture and movement screens**
5) **Joint flexibility and muscle length**: Sit-and-reach test
6) **Balance and core function**: Static and dynamic
7) **Cardiovascular Fitness**: Cycle ergometer tests; Ventilatory threshold testing; Field test (Rockport fitness 1 mile walking test, 1.5 mile run test); Step tests (YMCA submaximal step test)
8) **Muscular Fitness**: Muscular endurance (Push-up test, Curl-up test, Body-weight squat test) Muscular strength (1-RM testing for bench-press, leg-press & squat, Submaximal strength test)
9) **Skill-related assessments**: Balance, Agility, Coordination, Reaction time, Speed & Power.

Personal trainers must always be aware of signs or symptoms that merit immediate test termination when conducting any exercise test involving exertion with their clients and refer them to a qualified healthcare professional if necessary. Signs of serious health issues may not be present until the client exerts themselves. These signs and symptoms include the following:

- Onset of angina, chest pain, or angina-like symptoms
- Significant drop (>10 mmHg) in systolic blood pressure (SBP) despite an increase in exercise intensity
- Excessive rise in blood pressure (BP): SBP reaches >250 mmHg or diastolic blood pressure (DBP) reaches >115 mmHg
- Excess fatigue, shortness of breath, or wheezing *(does not include heavy breathing due to intense exercise)*
- Signs of poor perfusion: lightheadedness, pallor *(pale skin)*, cyanosis *(bluish coloration, especially around the mouth)*, nausea, or cold and clammy skin
- Increase nervous system symptoms *(e.g., ataxia, dizziness, confusion, or syncope)*
- Leg cramping or claudication
- Client request to stop
- Physical or verbal manifestations of severe fatigue
- Failure of testing equipment

Heart Rate Sites
1) Radial artery *(thumb side of wrist)*
2) Brachial *(anterior side of elbow)*
3) Carotid *(neck)*
Note the carotid artery is not the preferred site due to the possibility of reflexive slowing of the heart rate when pressed. Radial & Brachial are the locations of choice.

Body Composition: The relative proportion of lean tissue to body-fat tissue in the body.
*A certain amount of **essential body fat** is necessary, for men it's between 2 and 5% and for women it is between 10 and 13%.*

Lean Body Weight (LBW): The amount of fat-free weight (mass) one has.
Desired Body Weight (DBW) = Lean body weight ÷ (100% - Desired body fat %)

Body Fat Distribution: The location of fat on the body.
Waist to Hip ratio is a good indicator of body fat distribution. Waist ÷ Hip = WHR

Basal Metabolic Rate (BMR): Calories burned daily without movement.
To gain or lose weight one should increase or decrease calories by 300 to 400 kcals per day.

Body Mass Index (BMI): A weight to height ratio / BMI = Weight (Kg) ÷ Height (m^2)
***Note**: BMI cannot determine actual body composition, which means it can unfairly categorize some individuals (e.g. someone with a lot of muscle mass could be put in "obese" category).*

Height & Weight Conversions
1" = 2.54 cm
1 m = 100 cm
1 Kg = 2.2 pounds

Waist to Hip Ratio (WHR)
Waist circumference ÷ Hip circumference = Waist to Hip ratio
Health risk is high when above 0.95 for men & 0.86 for women
Health risk is high when waist circumference is ≥39.5" for men & ≥35.5" for women
Low risk is ≤31.5" for men & ≤27.5" for women
See Tables 8-10 & 8-11 on Pages 210 & 211 of American Council on Exercise Personal Trainer Manual - Fifth Edition.

Skinfold Measurement Locations
Use Chest, Thigh & Abdomen for men
Use Triceps, Thigh & Suprailium for women
Use Jackson and Pollock 3-site Skinfold Formulas to determine body fat percentage
See skinfold measurement locations starting with Figure 8-1 on Page 200 and skinfold measurement protocols on Page 202 of American Council on Exercise Personal Trainer Manual - Fifth Edition.

Skill related assessment considerations: The Pro agility test and 40-yard dash are both appropriate assessments for speed, agility and quickness testing. These tests along with power assessments *(Standing long jump test & Vertical jump test)* are designed for client's interested in performance training *(Phase 4 of the functional movement and resistance training component of the ACE IFT Model)*. The majority of normative data presented with these tests has been obtained from studies involving athletes. Little if any data exists for middle-aged or older adults. The results of these tests are best utilized as baseline data against which to measure a client's future performance. Keep in mind the majority of clients will not progress to this performance stage of training.

Muscular Fitness testing considerations: Submaximal strength testing can be used with a high amount of accuracy to determine a client's likely **one-repetition maximum (1-RM)**. 1-RM testing should only be performed during phase 3 or 4 of the ACE IFT Model due to the certain amount of risk involved with maximal exertion.

Cardiorespiratory Fitness (CRF): A person's ability to perform large muscle movement over a sustained period; related to the capacity of the heart-lung system to deliver oxygen for sustained energy production (Also called cardiorespiratory endurance or aerobic fitness).

Posture and Movement Term Definitions

Posture: The arrangement of the body and its limbs.
Static Posture: The alignment of the body's segments, how the person holds themselves "statically" with no movement in space.
Dynamic Posture: The position the body is in at any moment during a movement pattern.
Balance: The ability to maintain the body's position over its Base of Support (BOS) within stability limits, both statically and dynamically.
Static Balance: The ability to maintain the body's Center of Mass (COM) within its Base of Support (BOS)
Dynamic Balance: The act of maintaining postural control while moving.
Stability: Characteristic of the body's joints or posture that represents resistance to change of position.
Mobility: The degree to which an articulation is allowed to move before being restricted by surrounding tissues.

Static Posture Assessments

Postural deviations: Lordosis, Kyphosis, Flat back, Sway back, and Scoliosis.
(See Tables 7-1 thru 7-3 on Page 151 for muscle imbalances associated with these deviations and Figure 7-2 on Page 152 of American Council on Exercise Personal Trainer Manual - Fifth Edition for a diagram of these deviations)

Five key postural deviations that occur frequently: Ankle pronation/supination, Hip adduction, Pelvic tilting, Shoulder position and thoracic spine, and Head position.

*Postural deviations and muscle imbalance can be attributed to many correctible and non-correctible factors.

Correctible factors: Repetitive movements, awkward positions and movements *(poor posture)*, side dominance, lack of joint stability or mobility, and imbalanced resistance training programs.

Non-correctible factors: Congenital conditions *(scoliosis)*, some pathologies *(arthritis)*, structural deviations, and certain types of trauma *(surgery, injury, or amputation)*

*Note: When performing a static posture assessment on a client the personal trainer should focus on the obvious, gross imbalances and avoid over analyzing minor postural asymmetries.

Movement Observations & Assessments

* Familiarize yourself with the following screens. Know what they assess and ways to correct imbalances found. Information on all of these screens can be found starting on Page 167 and ending on Page 191 of American Council on Exercise Personal Trainer Manual - Fifth Edition.

Movement Screens: Bend and lift, Hurdle step, Shoulder push stabilization, Thoracic spine mobility *(See Figures 7-31 & 7-32 on Page 175).*

Flexibility and Muscle-Length testing: Thomas test for hip flexion/quadriceps length *(See Table 7-14 on Page 180)*, Passive straight-leg (PSL) raise, Shoulder mobility.

Balance and the Core: Sharpened Romberg test *(challenges the **vestibular system** by closing the eyes during test)*, Stork-Stand balance test, McGill's torso muscular endurance test battery.

Stability and Mobility points of the kinetic chain are described below:

Glenohumeral = Mobility
Scapulothoracic = Stability
Thoracic Spine = Mobility
Lumbar Spine = Stability
Hip = Mobility
Knee = Stability
Ankle = Mobility
Foot = Stability

***Proximal** stability promotes **Distal** mobility

Delayed activation of the **Transverse Abdominis (TVA)** may inadequately stabilize the lumbar spine during movements of the upper and lower extremities which increases the potential for injury. Individuals lacking proper TVA function tend to rely on synergistic muscles to stabilize the spine during movements. Altering the roles of the synergistic muscles for stabilization increases the potential for compromised function & injury.

Trainers must work to restore and maintain client's normal joint alignment, joint movement, muscle balance, and muscle function.

The principle of **"Straightening the body before strengthening it"** should be a priority of the personal trainer and client early in a training program. Adhering to this principle can improve the client's efficacy in their program and increase the likelihood of success in attaining their goals.

Skeleton & Spine

Axial Skeleton: Skull, Hyoid, Vertebral Column, Sternum & Ribs

Appendicular Skeleton: The remaining bones, mainly the bones of upper & lower limbs and their respective girdles.

Curves of the spine: Cervical, Thoracic, Lumbar, And Sacral

Kyphosis: Primary curves *(thoracic / sacral)*
Lordosis: Secondary curves *(cervical / lumbar)*
Scoliosis: Lateral deviation of the spine in the frontal plane.
Hyperkyphosis or Hyperlordosis: Deviations of the spine in the sagittal plane

There are **24** individual **vertebrae** in the spine:
7 Cervical (Neck)
12 Thoracic (Mid-back) *Ribs are connected to these*
5 Lumbar (Low-back)

We eat breakfast at 7, lunch at 12 and dinner at 5 is a good way to remember the vertebrae

Central Nervous System (CNS) is the brain & spinal cord.

Peripheral Nervous System (PNS) is other nerves throughout the body (somatic & visceral).

Types of Joints

There are three types of joints in the human body: Synarthrodial, Aamphiarthrodial & Diarthrodial *Synarthrodial (Synovial) joints move*

Types of Synovial Joints: Hinge, Ball & Socket

Hinge joints are formed between two or more bones where the bones can only move along one axis to flex or extend. *Ankle, Elbow & Knee joints are examples of hinge joints.*

Ball & Socket is a type of synovial joint where the ball-shaped surface of one bone fits into a cup-like depression of another bone. These joints are capable of moving on multiple axes from the common center of the ball joint. *Hip & Shoulder (Glenohumeral) joints are examples of ball & socket joints.*

Tendons link muscle & bone / ***Ligaments*** link bone to bone

Planes of Motion

It helps to visualize these & know which movements occur in each. A visual representation of the planes can be found on Page 99 Figure 5-4 of American Council on Exercise Personal Trainer Manual - Fifth Edition.

1 - **Sagittal plane**: Divides the body into the right & left sides. Forwards & backwards movements take place in the sagittal plane. *Bicep curls, bench press, walking & running are examples of movements in the Sagittal plane.*

2 - **Frontal plane**: Divides the body into anterior & posterior (front & back) portions. Vertical, left and right movements occur in the frontal plane. *Overhead press, abduction & adduction of the arms or legs while standing.*

3 - **Transverse plane**: Divides the body into superior & inferior (up / down) portions. Horizontal movements take place in the transverse plane.
Horizontal abduction/adduction or internal/external rotation of the arms.

Types of Movements

Open chain movements occur when distal segment (hand or foot) moves in space.
Bicep Curls, Lying triceps extensions, Leg extensions & Leg curls are examples of open chain movements.

Closed chain movements occur when distal segment is fixed in place.
Push-ups, Pull-ups, Squats, Deadlift & Lunges are examples of closed chain movements

Center of gravity (COG) is the point from which the weight of a body can be considered to act. The line of gravity is an imaginary vertical line passing through a person's COG. The line of gravity helps to define proper body alignment & posture using landmarks from the head to feet. COG changes with movement, body position & base of support. Proper body alignment during changes in COG will help to maintain form during exercise movements & help to prevent injuries.

Location Term Definitions

Inferior: Away from the head; lower
Superior: Toward the head; higher
Medial: Toward the midline of the body
Lateral: Away from the midline of the body; to the side
Proximal: Closer to any reference point
Distal: Farther from any reference point *(the hand is the distal segment when rotating the shoulder)*

Movement Term Definitions

Supination: Combined movements of adduction and inversion resulting in raising of the medial margin of the foot
Supine Position: Lying face up
Pronation: Combined movements of abduction and eversion resulting in lowering of the medial margin of the foot
Prone Position: Lying face down
Flexion: Movement involving a decrease in joint angle
Extension: Movement involving an increase in join angle
Adduction: Movement toward the midline of the body, usually in the frontal plane
Abduction: Movement away from the midline of the body, usually in the frontal plane
Hyperextension: Movement that extends the angle of a joint greater than normal
Rotation: Right or left twist in the transverse plane, usually used to describe neck & trunk movement.
Circumduction: A compound circular movement involving flexion, extension, abduction & adduction, circumscribing a cone shape

The Heart

There are four chambers of the heart: Right Atrium, Right Ventricle, Left Atrium, and Left Ventricle. *Think of these chambers as two separate pumps with two champers in each.*

The right side is responsible for collecting deoxygenated blood coming from the body & pumping this blood through the lungs. The left side collects the oxygenated blood from the lungs & pumps it to all parts of the body.

Blood flows through the heart chambers in the following order:
Right Atrium, Right Ventricle, Left Atrium, Left Ventricle

In addition to the heart chambers there are also four heart valves that maintain blood flow in a single direction. Blood flows through the valves in the following order:

Tricuspid Valve: Prevents backflow of blood into the right atrium.
Pulmonic Valve: Prevents backflow of blood into the right ventricle.
Mitral (Bicuspid) Valve: Prevents backflow of blood into the left atrium.
Aortic Valve: Prevents backflow of blood into the left ventricle.

The Sinoatrial (SA) node is the intrinsic pacemaker of the heart. This is where the electrical impulses of the heart originate.

The Atrioventricular (AV) node is responsible for delaying the electrical impulses from the SA node for approximately 0.12 seconds between the atria & the ventricles. This allows the right &

left atriums to contract & fill with blood. After a brief pause the electrical impulse moves through the heart bundle branches to contract the right & left ventricles at approximately the same time.

Heart Rate (HR)

Normal resting heart rate is between 60-100 BPM *(Beats per Minute)*.
The average resting heart rate is 70-72 BPM, averaging 60-70 BPM in males & 72-80 in females.
Sinus bradycardia: A heart rate that is slower than 60 BPM.
Sinus tachycardia: A heart rate that is faster than 100 BPM.

Resting heart rate (RHR) is influenced by fitness status, fatigue, body composition, body position, digestion, drugs and medication, alcohol, caffeine, and stress.

*Note certain drugs, medications and supplements can directly affect RHR. Clients should abstain from taking non-prescription stimulants or depressants for at least 12 hours prior to measuring their RHR.

*A person's true resting heart rate is measured just before they get out of bed in the morning.

A person with a lower resting heart rate may indicate a higher fitness level. An increase in stroke volume as a result of cardiovascular adaptations to exercise reduces the heart rate. Higher resting heart rates are indicative of poor physical fitness.

Knowing a client's resting heart rate (RHR) provides insight into target heart rates for training and signs of overtraining when their RHR is elevated more than 5 BPM over the course of a few days. Training intensity should decrease until the client recovers to their normal RHR.

Max Heart Rate (MHR): 220 – Age = MHR or 208 – (0.7 x Age) = MHR
*e.g. 30 year old would have Max HR of 190 BPM | 220 – 30 = 190 BPM

Heart Rate Reserve (HRR): Max HR – Resting HR = HRR
*e.g. 30 year old with resting HR of 60 BPM | 190 - 60 = 130 BPM

Target Heart Rate (THR) = HHR x % Intensity + Resting HR (Karoven Formula)
*e.g. 30 year old mentioned above to train at 80% intensity | 130 x 0.80 + 60 = 164 BPM (THR)

* HR increases in a linear fashion with exercise intensity.

Blood Pressure (BP)

Blood pressure is the result of the amount of blood pumped from the heart (cardiac output) and the resistance the flow of blood meets at the vessels. The force exerted by the blood against the arteries is the blood pressure.

Systolic blood pressure (SBP) is the pressure exerted on the arteries during the contraction phase of the heart (when the heart beats)

* SBP increases in a linear fashion with exercise intensity. A SBP that fails to rise or falls with increasing workloads may signal a plateau or decrease in cardiac output (Q).

Diastolic blood pressure (DBP) is the pressure exerted on the arteries during the relaxation phase of the heart (in between beats)

* DBP may decrease slightly or remain unchanged with exercise intensity.

The average value for systolic & diastolic blood pressure is 120/80 mm Hg (measured in millimeters of mercury)

Hypertension (high blood pressure) is when systolic & diastolic blood pressure meets or exceeds 140/90 mm Hg at rest.

Stroke Volume (SV)

Stoke volume is the amount of blood ejected from the left ventricle of the heart in a single contraction. SV is lower in an upright posture (standing up) in untrained individuals compared to trained individuals. SV also increases in the supine or prone positions (lying down).

During dynamic exercise SV increases curvilinearly with intensity. SV reaches near maximal levels approximately at 40% to 50% of maximum aerobic capacity. Once SV reaches its maximum levels, the increase in oxygen demand is met by increasing the heart rate.

Cardiac Output (Q)

Cardiac output is the amount of blood pumped by the heart per minute in liters. It is calculated using the following formula: Heart Rate (HR) x Stroke Volume (SV) = Cardiac Output (Q)

* Cardiac output (Q) increases in a linear fashion with exercise intensity.

Muscles

Three types of muscle: Skeletal, Cardiac, Smooth

Muscles fiber types: Type I (slow twitch), Type II (fast twitch), Type IIx (intermediate)
Type IIx is a hybrid with both fast twitch (explosive) & slow twitch (endurance) capabilities.

The muscles fibers that are recruited to perform exercise are the only ones stimulated to adapt. Low-intensity endurance exercise usually causes adaptations in the Type I *(slow-twitch)* muscle fibers whereas higher-intensity exercise causes more Type II *(fast-twitch)* muscle fibers to be recruited. The adaptations that occur enhance energy production. Hypertrophy occurs when the recruitment reaches the upper limit of a muscles capacity to generate force.

Muscles that act primarily as stabilizers generally contain greater concentrations of Type I *(slow-twitch, endurance)* muscle fibers. The core muscles are an example of this as they stabilize the spine during loading and movement throughout the day. Stabilizer muscles are better suited for endurance-type training *(higher-volume, lower-intensity)*

Muscles primarily responsible for joint movement generally contain greater concentrations of Type II *(fast-twitch, explosive)* muscle fibers. These muscles are better suited for strength and power-type training *(higher-intensity, lower-volume)*

The smallest contractile unit of a muscle fiber *(cell)* is called a **Sarcomere**. Sarcomeres are made up of two types of muscle protein: **Actin** *(thin filament)* & **Myosin** *(thick filament)*

Myofibril is the portion of the muscle containing the thick (myosin) and thin (actin) contractile filaments; a series of sarcomeres where the repeating pattern of the contractile proteins gives the striated appearance to skeletal muscle.

Length-Tension Relationship is the relationship between the contractile proteins *(actin & myosin)* of a sarcomere and their force-generating capacity. When a muscle is shortened due to bad posture *(passive shortening)*, immobilization, trauma or aging there is a loss in the number of sarcomeres within the myofibril of the muscle fiber. This reduces force-generating capacity in the normal and lengthened muscle positions. Muscles can shorten in as little as 2-4 weeks when held in passively shortened positions. Passive stretching or elongation of a tightened muscle done on a regular basis will gradually add sarcomeres back in line and help restore the normal resting length of a muscle.

Muscle spindles sense any stretching or tension within a muscle; their main function is to respond to the stretch of a muscle and through a reflex action initiate a stronger muscle action *(contraction)* to reduce the stretch, called **"Stretch reflex"**.

Golgi tendon organs (GTO) attach to the tendons near the junction of the muscle. They detect differences in tension & when excessive tension is detected they send a signal to prevent the muscle from contracting to prevent muscle injury resulting from over-contraction.

Autogenic inhibition is a principle stating that activation of a Golgi tendon organ (GTO) inhibits a muscle spindle response. An initial static stretch *(low-force)* causes a temporary increase in muscle tension *(low-grade)*. As the stretch is held a **stress-relaxation response** occurs gradually releasing tension. After 7-10 seconds of a low-force stretch the increase in muscle tension activates a GTO response. After this response the muscle spindle tension is temporarily inhibited allowing further muscle stretching. The lengthening that occurs beyond 10 seconds of holding a stretch is called **creep**.

A **monoarticulate** muscle crosses one joint. A **biarticulate** muscle crosses two joints.

Muscle Action Definitions

Concentric: Shortening portion of muscle contraction. *(Moving external resistance)*
Eccentric: Lengthening phase of muscle contraction. *(Control during lengthening portion of movement against force)*
Isometric: Static, muscle stays in same place against external load. *(Joints do not move)*
Isotonic: Same tone throughout movement
Isokinetic: Same speed throughout movement
*Muscle actions involving joint movement are considered dynamic

Muscle Term Definitions

Agonist: Prime mover (muscle) during movement *(biceps are agonist during bicep curl)*
Antagonist: Opposing muscles during movement *(triceps are antagonist during bicep curl)*
Stabilizer: Muscles that stabilize a joint or portion of the body against a force
Synergist: Muscles that prevent unwanted joint movement & help prime movers (agonist) perform more efficiently
Hypertrophy: Increase in size of muscle fibers
Hyperplasia: Increase in number of muscle fibers
Atrophy: Decrease in muscle fibers
DOMS: Delayed Onset Muscle Soreness

Rotator Cuff Muscles: Supraspinatus, Infraspinatus, Teres minor, Subscapularis (**SITS**)

Supraspinatus: Abducts the glenohumeral (shoulder) joint
Infraspinatus: Externally rotates the glenohumeral (shoulder) joint
Teres minor: Externally rotates the glenohumeral (shoulder) joint
Subscapularis: Internally rotates the glenohumeral (shoulder) joint

Quadriceps Muscles: Rectus femoris, Vastus lateralis, Vastus intermedius, Vastus medialis

Hamstring Muscles: Biceps femoris (long & short heads), Semitendinosus, Semimembranosus

Domain II: Program Design & Implementation

Create client programs that focus on healthy lifestyles through the development of individualized physical activity, nutrition, and education necessary to improve and maintain health, fitness, weight, body composition and metabolism.

Common Resistance-Training Myths & Mistakes

- Fat deposits in certain areas (e.g., the abdomen or thighs) can be targeted with strength training via spot reduction. Remember the phrase "First on, last off" fat deposits come off in the reverse order that they were stored.
- Women will build bulky muscles through weight training.
- Individuals should use light weights and high repetitions to improve muscle tone, and heavy weights and low repetitions to increase muscle mass.
- At some point, people get too old to lift weights.
- Children are too young to lift weights.
- Free weights are always better than machines.
- After a person stops resistance training, the muscle turns to fat.
- Strength training is bad for the exercisers blood pressure.

***Note**: Additional information can be found on Pages 382 thru 385 of American Council on Exercise Personal Trainer Manual - Fifth Edition.*

Training Principles

Specificity of training: Only the muscles that are trained will adapt and change in response.

SAID Principles: Specific Adaptations to Imposed Demands

Progressive overload: As the body adapts to a given stimulus, an increase in stimulus is required for further adaptations and improvements. Increasing repetitions and adding resistance in **5% increments** *(whenever the end range number of reps can be completed)* are two principal approaches to strength-training progression.
*__Note__: To maximize strength devolvement, the resistance should be heavy enough to fatigue the target muscles within the limits of the **anaerobic energy system** (90 seconds or less).*

FITT-VP: Frequency, Intensity, Time, Type, Volume, Progression
The FITT-VP principles should be used to design Cardiorespiratory, Muscular & Flexibility exercise programs

FIRST: Frequency, Intensity, Repetitions, Sets and Type

Term Definitions

Microcycle: The smallest training cycle time frame in a periodization program. This cycle usually ranges from 2 – 4 weeks in length & focuses on one type of workout variable in that phase.
Mesocycle: The middle group of training cycle time frames in a periodization program. Combining these makes up the larger macrocycle, usually 4 – 6 mesocycles per year.
Macrocycle: The largest training cycle time frame of a periodization program (6 – 12 months). This cycle consist of the combined micro & mesocycles.
Multi-joint exercise: Involves two or more muscle groups & joints during the exercise. *(Dead lifts, squats & bench press are examples of multi-joint exercises)*
Single-joint exercise: Isolated muscle group exercises involving one joint movement. *(Bicep curls, knee extensions & leg curls are some examples of single-joint exercises)*
Unilateral: Exercises or movements involving one limb. *(One arm bicep curl is an example)*
Bilateral: Exercises or movements involving both limbs. *(Barbell bench press is an example)*
Push exercises: Exercises involving the "push" muscle groups. *(Bench press, squats & abduction)*
Pull exercises: Exercises involving the "pull" muscle groups. *(Pull ups, dead lifts & adduction)*

Types of Training Programs

High Intensity Interval Training (HIIT): Alternating brief periods of high-intensity activity followed by less intense recovery periods. This type of training produces greater benefits in a shorter amount of "training" time. Benefits include improved speed, endurance, recovery time, cardiovascular health, insulin sensitivity, fat burning & increased metabolism. Interval training should not be performed on consecutive days to reduce the potential for overtraining. Typically performing HIIT on 2-3 non-consecutive days per week is sufficient.
*Note: Interval training promotes greater improvements in VO_2 Max and lactate threshold enhancing a person's ability to sustain higher intensities of exercise for longer periods.

Steady State Training: Involves activity without rest intervals. This type of training can be performed at low, moderate or high intensities. Continuous training improves aerobic fitness, endurance & aids in weight loss. This type of training is more time consuming than interval or circuit training & also does very little for anaerobic fitness.

Circuit Training: Involves performing several continuous exercises in a short period of time. This type of training induces metabolic and cardiovascular responses that could improve aerobic capacity. It also targets strength building & muscular endurance.

Plyometric Training: Explosive exercises that target power development. These exercises begin with a quick stretch of the muscle fibers (eccentric phase) followed by a fast shortening of the same muscle fibers (concentric phase). Jump lunges, box jumps & sprints are some examples of plyometric training.
*Note: Clients should not jump unless they are capable of landing correctly. Teaching clients small, low-intensity jumps with appropriate landing techniques will help to avoid injuries.

Super setting: Consecutive performance of two exercises either for the same or different muscle groups.

Olympic lifting: Total body resistance exercises that recruit most major muscle groups. Olympic lifts are the most complex exercises to perform but also are considered the most effective for increasing total-body power. The clean and jerk, snatch & overhead squats are some examples.

Variation in training: No one program should be used without changing the exercise stimulus over time.

Periodization: The phasic manipulation of training variables (volume, intensity, frequency, and rest intervals) as means of optimizing desired physiological outcomes while reducing the incidence of overtraining. Periodization allows for optimal training and recovery time.

Linear periodization: Steady linear increase in intensity of a program. A traditional linear periodization program contains the following four phases:
1) Hypertrophy phase (high volume, short rest periods)
2) Strength / power phase (reduced volume but increased resistance and rest periods)
3) Peaking phase (low volume but high resistance & longer rest periods)
4) Recovery phase (low volume & low resistance)

Nonlinear (Undulating) periodization: Allows for variation in the intensity and volume over the course of a training program.

Training Considerations

The initial stage of an exercise program should consist of low intensity exercises for clients who are new to resistance training. Progressing a beginner client too quickly to higher intensity exercises could cause **delayed onset muscle soreness (DOMS)** or injury and reduce their adherence to regular exercise. Designing an exercise program that begins at a low level of intensity then gradually progresses intensity as the client physically and psychologically adapts to the training stress increases results and long-term exercise adherence.

Training sessions should include the following three components:

Warm-up: At least 5-10 minutes of low to moderate cardio & muscular endurance activities.
*Dynamic stretching, Body weight movements, elliptical, treadmill or other cardio equipment.
Conditioning: At least 20-60 minutes of aerobic, resistance, neuromotor and/or sports specific activities.
Cool-down: At least 5-10 minutes of low to moderate cardio & muscular endurance activities.
*Stretching, Body weight movements, decompressing from the workout.

There are six motor skill related components of physical fitness: Agility, Balance, Coordination, Reaction time, Speed & Power.

All training programs should be developed to meet specific client needs. Each resistance exercise has a certain amount of transfer to another activity, referred to as **"transfer specificity"**. Sports specific exercises should transfer specificity at the highest rate possible; however training is only 100% transferred when performing the exact targeted task *(playing baseball, basketball, soccer, etc....)*

Detraining or reversibility of conditioning refers to when training stimulus is stopped the body gradually returns to its pre-conditioned state. It is a partial or complete reversal of the physiological adaptations gained through exercise. The phrase "Use it or Lose it" is a simple way to remember this concept.

Rhabdomyolysis: Often a sign of overtraining this condition happens when a rapid breakdown of muscle tissue results in the release of intramuscular proteins (myoglobin, myosin protein) into the bloodstream. This can be potentially harmful to the kidneys and could lead to kidney failure and sometimes death in extreme cases.

Valsalva maneuver: Moderate forceful exhalation against a closed airway (close mouth, pinch nose shut) while pressing out as if blowing up a balloon. The Valsalva maneuver is commonly used in powerlifting to stabilize the trunk during exercises like the squat & deadlift. The Valsalva maneuver should be avoided by the general population as it increases intra-abdominal pressure, blood pressure & heart rate. This can be dangerous by hindering a person's cardiac output & cause dizziness or fainting.

The **one rep max (1RM)** test is beneficial to determine training loads for exercises where going to failure or near failure is not practical *(Power cleans, Olympic-style lifts)*. Once the 1RM is known a percentage of that max is used to determine optimal training load for a given exercise (e.g. 70% - 85% of 1RM). One rep max estimates based on repetitions are listed in table below.

Repetitions	% of 1RM
1	100
2	95
3	93
4	90
5	87
6	85
7	83
8	80
9	77
10	75
11	70
12	67
15	65

Training Volume Based on Goals

A person's current fitness status provides a good indicator of the appropriate volume. Deconditioned or novice clients should begin with manageable volumes prior to progressing to the training volumes outlined below. Advanced individuals may require additional Frequency, Intensity, Time and Volume in order to obtain progressive results.

General Muscle Fitness
Sets: 1-2 per exercise
Reps: 8-15 per set
Rest: 30-90 seconds between sets
Intensity: Varies

Endurance
Sets: 2-3 per exercise
Reps: ≥12 per set
Rest: ≤30 seconds between sets
Intensity: 60 to 70% of 1RM

Hypertrophy
Sets: 3-6 per exercise
Reps: 6-12 per set
Rest: 30-90 seconds between sets
Intensity: 70 to 90% of 1RM

Strength
Sets: 2-6 per exercise
Reps: ≤6 per set
Rest: 2-5 minutes between sets
Intensity: 80 to 90% of 1RM

Power
Sets: 3-5 per exercise
Reps: 1-2 per set for Single-effort events / 3-5 per set for multiple-effort events
Rest: 2-5 minutes between sets
Intensity: >90% of 1RM

* **Isometric** exercises strengthen muscle within **15 degrees** of the position held.

* The most effective training programs use concentric-eccentric repetitions.

Methods of Estimating Exercise Intensity

VO_2 Max: Maximal oxygen consumption
With training VO_2 Max increases but reaches a peak and plateaus within about six months.
VO_2 Rest: Resting oxygen consumption (VO_2 Rest = 3.5)
VO_2 Reserve: Oxygen uptake reserve (VO_2 Reserve = VO_2 Max - 3.5)
Target VO_2 = VO_2 Max - VO_2 Rest x % of Intensity + VO_2 Rest
__Note__: Training programs based on % of VO_2 Max or VO_2 Reserve depend on an accurate maximal or submaximal exercise test to determine a person's true VO_2 Max. Given that maximal test are rarely available and equations for estimating VO_2 Max are not 100% accurate this technique is not recommended unless a person's VO_2 Max is directly measured.

MET: Metabolic Energy Equivalent
MET is an index of energy expenditure. One MET is the rate of energy expenditure while at rest that is equal to an oxygen uptake (VO_2) of 3.5
$VO_2 \div 3.5$ = MET
MET x 3.5 x Body Weight in Kg ÷ 200 = kcal (Calories expended per minute formula)
See Table 11-6 on Page 406 of American Council on Exercise Personal Trainer Manual Fifth Edition for common physical activities MET values.

Max Heart Rate (MHR): 220 – Age = MHR or 208 – (0.7 x Age) = MHR
e.g. 30 year old would have Max HR of 190 BPM | 220 – 30 = 190 BPM

Heart Rate Reserve (HRR): Max HR – Resting HR = HRR
e.g. 30 year old with resting HR of 60 BPM | 190 - 60 = 130 BPM

Target Heart Rate (THR) = HHR x % Intensity + Resting HR (Karoven Formula)
e.g. 30 year old mentioned above to train at 80% intensity | 130 x 0.80 + 60 = 164 BPM (THR)

Ratings of Perceived Exertion (RPE): 0-10 point (modern scale) or 6-20 point (classic scale)
Table 6-5 on Page 144 of American Council on Exercise Personal Trainer Manual Fifth Edition.

__Note__: Due to the standard deviations in estimating a person's max heart rate (MHR), Training heart rate should be used in combination with the ratings of perceived exertion (RPE) scale.

Ventilatory Threshold is the point of transition between predominately aerobic energy production to anaerobic energy production. With regular exercise a person's ventilatory or lactate threshold can increase for some time beyond their primary increase in VO_2 Max. The **first ventilatory threshold (VT1)** or "crossover" point represents a level of intensity at which blood lactate accumulates faster than it can be cleared, which causes the person to breathe faster in an effort to blow off the extra CO_2 produced. The "talk test" *(if a person can talk comfortably in sentences while performing the exercise)* is a good indicator that someone is training below VT1. The **second ventilatory threshold (VT2)** occurs at the point of intensity where blowing off the CO_2 is no longer adequate to buffer the rapidly increasing lactate. High-intensity exercise *(≥VT2)* can only be sustained for a brief period due to the accumulation of lactate. A person's heart rate can be determined at both VT1 and VT2 thresholds by using the Submaximal talk test for VT1 and VT2 threshold testing.

***Note**: VT2 threshold test should only be performed by clients who are at low to moderate risk and who are successfully training in Phase 3 (Anaerobic Endurance) of the ACE IFT Model.
For additional information on ventilatory threshold testing see Pages 221 & 222 of American Council on Exercise Personal Trainer Manual - Fifth Edition.

VT1 & VT2 metabolic markers can be used to divide training intensity into the following 3 zones.

- Zone 1 (low to moderate exercise) reflects heart rates below VT1
- Zone 2 (moderate to vigorous exercise) reflects heart rates above VT1 to just below VT2
- Zone 3 (vigorous to very vigorous exercise) reflects heart rates at or above VT2

Energy Systems

Adenosine triphosphate (ATP) is a high-energy compound required to do all mechanical work produced by the human body.

Muscle fibers produce ATP by three pathways: Creatine phosphate (CP), Anaerobic Glycolysis & Aerobic Oxidation.

Anaerobic energy systems do not require oxygen to produce energy. They are the immediate short-term systems used in the first few minutes of exercise. ATP stored in muscle, Creatine Phosphate (PCr) & Anaerobic Glycolysis make up the anaerobic energy systems.

The Aerobic system requires oxygen to produce energy. It uses carbohydrates, fats & proteins to produce ATP. Carbohydrates are the primary source of energy at the onset of exercise & during high-intensity work followed by fats during prolonged exercise of low to moderate intensity *(longer than 30 minutes)* & then proteins.

Energy Pathways

ATP: 0-4 Seconds (Strength & Power)
**Uses ATP stored in muscles*

ATP+PCr: 0-10 seconds (Sustained Power)

ATP+PCr+Lactic Acid: 0-90 seconds (Anaerobic Power-Endurance)

Aerobic Oxidation: 90 seconds to 3+ minutes (Aerobic Endurance)

ACE Integrated Fitness Training Model (ACE IFT)

The following provides a brief summary of The ACE IFT Model which is a registered trademark of the American Council on Exercise. For additional information see Chapters 5 thru 12 of American Council on Exercise Personal Trainer Manual - Fifth Edition.

The **Function-Health-Fitness-Performance Continuum** states that exercise programs should follow a progression to first reestablish proper function, then improve health, then develop and advance fitness, and finally enhance performance.

The ACE IFT Model has two principal training components that are divided into four phases based on the Function-Health-Fitness-Performance Continuum:

Functional movement and resistance training: (Phase 1 Function) Stability and Mobility Training, (Phase 2 Health) Movement Training, (Phase 3 Fitness) Load Training, (Phase 4) Performance Training.

Cardiorespiratory training: (Phase 1 Function) Aerobic-base Training, (Phase 2 Health) Aerobic-efficiency Training, (Phase 3 Fitness) Anaerobic-endurance Training, (Phase 4 Performance) Anaerobic-power Training.

The ACE IFT Model allows trainers to develop individualized programs for clients ranging from sedentary to athletes. Clients are categorized into a given phase based on their current health, fitness levels, and goals.

Programming in each phase will be based on the <u>three-zone training model</u> shown in Figure 11-6 on Page 410 of American Council on Exercise Personal Trainer Manual - Fifth Edition.

***Note**: Clients may be in different phases for cardiorespiratory and functional movement and resistance training based on their current health, fitness, exercise-participation levels, and goals.*

Table 5-4 & Figure 5-3 describing the ACE IFT Model and its components can be found on Page 95 of American Council on Exercise Personal Trainer Manual - Fifth Edition.

Table 11-8 on Page 420 of American Council on Exercise Personal Trainer Manual - Fifth Edition shows the three-zone training model using various intensity markers.

***Rapport** is the foundation for success for all phases of the ACE IFT Model.*

Functional Movement and Resistance Training

Phase 1: Stability and Mobility Training

Assessments of the client's posture, balance, movement, range of motion of the ankle, hip, shoulder complex, and thoracic and lumbar spine should be performed in the early stages of this phase of training. The personal trainer can then implement an exercise program that addresses the client's weaknesses and imbalances found during these assessments. The goal of this phase is to develop the client's postural stability and proper movement patterns.

Proximal Stability

It is recommended this training phase begin with the establishment of proximal stability within the lumbar spine region, which encompasses the body's **Center of Mass (COM)** and the core. Focus on exercises that emphasize **Transverse Abdominis (TVA)** activation *(drawing the belly button toward the spine "centering")* and the re-education of potentially faulty motor patterns to improve reflexive function of the core musculature.

Proximal Mobility

The goal of this stage is to improve mobility of the two joints immediately adjacent to the lumbar spine (Hips and Thoracic Spine). Exercises should be performed to promote mobility of these two regions in all three planes (Sagittal, Frontal & Transverse) focusing on the muscles primary plane of movement first.

Phase 2: Movement Training

Five primary human movement patterns: Bend-and-lift movements, Single-leg movements, Pushing movements, Pulling Movements, Rotational Movements

When teaching clients bend-and-lift or single-leg movements the trainer should begin with "arms down" positions as "high-arm" positions require a greater degree of thoracic mobility which many clients may lack.

The need for thoracic mobility is greater during rotational movements given the three-dimensional nature of the movement patterns. Performing these movements without proper thoracic mobility or lumbar stability may compromise the shoulders and hips increasing the likelihood of injury.

Trainers should always incorporate stability and mobility training during the initial phase of a client's training program. Restoring good joint alignment and muscle balance along with proper execution of the five primary movement patterns is the foundation to all movement.

If resistance is added to dysfunctional movement patterns, it increases the risk of injury.

Before adding resistance to movement patterns the client must first demonstrate proficiency with the following: Performing body-weight movement sequences with proper form, Core stabilization, Control of their center of gravity (COG), Control of the velocity of movement.

Balance is the foundational element of all programming. Movement is essential to complete all activities of daily living (ADL), and the ability to move efficiently requires balance (control of the body's postural alignment). *Balance is a trainable skill and improvements are evident within a few weeks.*

Activities of daily living (ADL) are basic daily tasks such as self-care and household chores. One's ability to perform these tasks has been correlated with balance, postural control & joint mobility. Flexibility exercises along with resistance training can help to improve range of motion (ROM) within the joints as well as increase balance and postural stability.

Motor learning is the process of acquiring and improving motor skills. Many adult clients will demonstrate a lack of motor ability especially in the early stages of a training program. Clients must be reminded that it takes time and practice to improve motor skills. Introducing new skills slowly and clearly along with providing reassurance will help clients gain confidence over time.

Stages of Learning: Cognitive, Associative, and Autonomous

As clients try to understand a new skill they are in the initial **Cognitive** stage of learning. In the **Associative** stage of learning clients begin to master the basics and are ready for specific feedback that will help them refine the motor skill. Clients are then performing motor skills effectively and naturally in the final **Autonomous** stage of learning.

Phase 3: Load Training

This phase of load training is used to enhance muscle hypertrophy, strength & endurance. **Muscle hypertrophy** is the increase in size of muscle fibers. **Muscular strength** is the ability of a muscle or muscle group to exert force *(usually measured by one-repetition maximum 1-RM)*. **Muscular endurance** is the ability of a muscle or muscle group to continually perform without fatigue *(measured by repeated or sustained muscle contractions)*. Load training should be manipulated using the ***FITT-VP principles*** to achieve the clients desired exercise goals *(positive changes in body composition, muscular strength, muscular endurance, muscle hypertrophy, looking more "toned", etc.)*

FITT-VP: Frequency, Intensity, Time, Type, Volume, Pattern / Progressions

General FITT-VP recommendations for resistance exercise can be found in Table 5-3 on Page 91 of American Council on Exercise Personal Trainer Manual - Fifth Edition.

Frequency: Each major muscle group should be trained 2-3 days per week.
Intensity: Varies depending on fitness level and individual goals.
Time: No specific duration of training has been identified for effectiveness.
Type: Resistance exercises involving each major muscle group are recommended. Multi-joint and Single-joint exercises can be used with a variety of exercise equipment and/or body weight.
Volume: Repetitions and sets vary depending on fitness level and individual goals.
Pattern: Rest intervals of 2-3 minutes between each set of repetitions are effective. A rest of ≥48 hours between sessions for any single muscle group is recommended.
Progression: A gradual progression of greater resistance, and/or more repetitions per set, and/or increasing frequency is recommended.

Phase 4: Performance Training

Performance training programs are designed to improve the motor skill related components of physical fitness including speed, agility, quickness, reactivity, and power. Clients who progress to this stage of training should continue to incorporate stability, mobility and movement training as part of dynamic warm-ups to maintain postural stability and proper movement patterns. Clients should have the following prerequisites for performance training:

- A foundation of strength and joint integrity (joint mobility and stability)
- Adequate static and dynamic balance
- Effective core function
- Anaerobic efficiency (training of the anaerobic pathways)
- Athleticism (sufficient skills to perform advanced movements)
- No **contraindications** to load-bearing, dynamic movements
- No medical concerns that affect balance and motor skills

Cardiorespiratory Training

Table 11-9 on Page 422 of American Council on Exercise Personal Trainer Manual - Fifth Edition provides an overview of the cardiorespiratory training phases of the ACE IFT Model.

Phase 1: Aerobic-base Training

This phase is designed to develop an Aerobic-base for clients who have been sedentary or near-sedentary. This training phase establishes the foundation for aerobic fitness and health that is built upon in the following stages. Exercise during this phase should be performed at steady-state intensities in the low-to-moderate range. The goal of this phase is to gradually increase duration and frequency until the client is performing cardiorespiratory exercise 3-5 days per week for a duration of 20-30 minutes at a **rating of perceived exertion RPE** of 3-4. The best method for monitoring intensity during this phase is by using the **talk test** *(if a client can talk comfortably in sentences while performing the exercise)* likely keeping them below the **first ventilatory threshold (VT1)**.

***Note**: Cardiorespiratory fitness assessments are not recommended during this phase.*

Phase 2: Aerobic-efficiency Training

This phase is designed to enhance the client's aerobic efficiency by increasing exercise duration, frequency (when possible), and introducing aerobic intervals. Aerobic intervals are introduced at a level that is at or just above VT1, or an RPE of 5 (strong) on a 0-10 point scale. The goal of aerobic intervals is to improve aerobic endurance and increase the client's ability to use fat as a fuel source.

Phase 3: Anaerobic-endurance Training

The primary focus of this stage is to design programs that improve performance in endurance and achieve higher levels of cardiorespiratory fitness. Higher-intensity intervals are introduced to load the cardiorespiratory system enough to develop anaerobic endurance. Lactate threshold or tolerance training increases the amount of sustained work that an individual can perform at or near the **second ventilatory threshold (VT2)**. The phase 3 training zones should be used for this phase *(Table 5-5 on Page 105 of American Council on Exercise Personal Trainer Manual - Fifth Edition)* by alternating time spent below VT1, between VT1 & VT2, and at or above VT2. The importance of recovery for improving fitness and performance should be emphasized to the client, especially if signs of overtraining are present *(increased resting heart rate, disturbed, sleep, or decreased hunger on multiple days)*. The training sessions in this stage should occur at a rate that allows the client ample recovery time to prepare their body for the next session.

Phase 4: Anaerobic-power Training

This phase is designed to build on the training done in the previous 3 phases and introduce short-duration, high-intensity intervals designed to enhance anaerobic power. Intervals in this stage performed well above VT2 or an RPE of 9 (very, very strong) will help to develop peak power and aerobic power. Overloading the fast glycolytic system and challenging the phosphagen system will enhance the client's ability to perform high-intensity work for extended periods. Longer recovery periods are necessary in this phase to prevent overtraining. Phase 4 training zones can be found in Table 5-6 on Page 106 of *American Council on Exercise Personal Trainer Manual - Fifth Edition*.

Mind-Body Exercise

Mind-body exercise is low to moderate-intensity physical activity performed with a meditative, proprioceptive, or sensory-awareness component (physical exercise executed with a profound inward mental focus).

Muscle afferents are neurons that conduct impulses from sensory receptors into the central nervous system (CNS). Figures 13-1 & 13-2 on Page 482 of *American Council on Exercise Personal Trainer Manual - Fifth Edition* describe how muscle afferent pathways carry sensory information from the muscles & joints to the brain forming a body-mind conduit.

Mind-body exercise can assist in the management of a number of chronic disease states, including cardiovascular disease (CVD), diabetes, and arthritis. In order for a yoga (mind-body) program to cause regression or slow the progression of coronary disease there must be a significant modification of blood lipids and lipoproteins (LDL cholesterol), primarily achieved by dietary means. A healthy "yogic lifestyle" rather than yoga alone is necessary for generating significant changes.

Stretching Techniques

Static: Slowly move into position then holding that stretch at the point of tightness for 15 – 60 seconds. Repeat for a minimum of 4 repetitions.

Dynamic: Moving parts of the body through a full ROM while gradually increasing the reach and/or speed of that movement in a controlled manner progressing from smaller to larger ROM. Great to use during warm up or as part of the cool down.

Ballistic: Involves a bouncing or jerky type movement to reach the muscle's ROM limits. Ballistic stretching is not appropriate for the general population.

Passive: Person stretching is not actively involved. The person assumes a position and then either holds it with another part of the body or with assistance from a partner or some other apparatus (resistance band, towel, etc.….)

Proprioceptive Neuromuscular Facilitation (PNF): A method of promoting the response of neuromuscular mechanisms through the stimulation of proprioceptors in an attempt to gain more stretch in a muscle. PNF involves both stretching and contracting the targeted muscle group. Once in position a person holds a 20% - 75% voluntary contraction for a minimum of 6 seconds, followed by 10 – 30 seconds of assisted stretch.

Myofascial release: A manual massage technique used to eliminate general fascial restrictions; typically performed with a device such as a foam roller.

Fascia are strong connective tissues that perform a number of functions, including developing and isolating the muscles of the body and providing structural support and protection. Plural form is ***Fasciae***.

Three types of stretching to improve ROM: Static, Dynamic & PNF.

Stretching should be done 2-3 days per week but is most effective when performed daily.

***Note**: Static stretches should be avoided before resistance training. Dynamic stretches can be done prior to resistance training.*

Movements of major muscle groups (Biomechanics)

Biomechanics is the study of motion and causes of motion of living things.

Biomechanical principles should be used during common physical activities such as walking, running, lifting and carrying objects as well as resistance training.

Squats are a full body multi-joint compound exercise. The gluteus maximus & quadriceps are the agonist (prime movers) and the hamstrings, erector spinae, transverse abdominis, gluteus medius/minimus, abductors, adductors, soleus & gastrocnemius are the synergists & stabilizer (secondary) muscles involved during the squat.

The deadlift is another compound movement that works a variety of muscle groups. The erector spinae (lower back) are the agonist along with gluteus maximus and hamstrings to extend the hip joint. The quadriceps also works to extend the knee joint. The adductor magnus works to stabilize the legs. The forearms & grip muscles of the hands hold the bar. The core muscles activate to help the erector spinae stabilize the spine during the movement.

The bench press is an upper body compound movement. The agonist muscles of the bench press are pectoralis major & minor, anterior deltoids & triceps. The antagonist muscles of the bench press are the biceps, posterior deltoids, rhomboids & trapezius.

Proper form, technique and control are essential during these compound movements to prevent injury & optimize the targeted muscles worked.

Spotting Techniques

Proper spotting techniques reassure the client while performing an exercise & reduce the risk of injury during that exercise. Verbal explanation along with a demonstration of proper lifting technique & form by the personal trainer prior to the client performing the actual exercise will help the client to understand and maintain proper position, form, technique and control. A trainer should use common sense when spotting a client by staying close when needed in a proper spotting position, keeping hands on or close to weight being lifted, know how many repetitions the lifter intends to do, stop lifters if they break form or have improper technique, make sure to have a good base of support & are strong enough to assist the lifter with the resistance being used. Remember to always ask your clients before physically touching them to ensure they are comfortable with it.

e.g. During a barbell back squat the spotter should stand behind the lifter with their hands up and under the armpits of the lifter (not touching unless necessary) while moving up and down with the lifter (in a similar motion as the squat itself).

Nutrition & Human Performance

There are 6 classes of nutrients: Carbohydrates, Fats, Protein, Vitamins, Minerals & Water

Macronutrients: Carbohydrates, Fats & Protein *these are the energy sources for our body*

Micronutrients: Vitamins & Minerals

Fat soluble nutrients: Vitamins A, D, E & K

Water soluble nutrients: Vitamins B, C & Niacin

Minerals: Calcium, Phosphorus, Iron, Zinc & Magnesium

There are **20 amino acids** found in the human body, **9 essential** & **11 nonessential**.
The body cannot produce essential amino acids so they must be obtained from the foods we eat whereas nonessential amino acids can be produced by the body.

Types of Fat

Long chain: Contains 14 or more carbon atoms
Medium chain: Contains 8-12 carbon atoms *Medium chain triglycerides (MCT) are an excellent source of fuel for the body where as long chain fatty acids cannot be used as fuel.*
Short chain: Contains 6 or less carbon atoms
Polyunsaturated: Helps lower blood cholesterol levels
Monounsaturated: Helps lower blood cholesterol levels while maintaining HDL
High-density lipoproteins (HDL): Carry lipids away from storage into the liver for metabolism and/or excretion. They are considered "good cholesterol"
Low-density lipoproteins (LDL): The major carrier of cholesterol & other lipids in the blood.

Kilocalorie (Calorie) Breakdown

Fat = 9 calories per gram
Protein = 4 calories per gram
Carbohydrates = 4 calories per gram
Alcohol = 7 calories per gram
3500 kcal (calories) = 1 pound of fat

Daily Macronutrient Recommendations

Carbohydrates: 6 to 10 grams per kilogram of body weight per day (45% - 65% of total calories)

Protein: 0.8 grams per kilogram of body weight per day for adults (10% - 35% of total calories)
Adult athletes range from 1.2 to 1.7 g per kg of body weight

Fats: 20% to 35% of total calories

Fluid & Hydration

The following are fluid-intake recommendations during exercise:

- Drink 500-600 mL (17-20 oz) 2 hours prior to exercise
- Drink 200-300 mL (7-10 oz) every 10-20 minutes during exercise or preferably, drink based on sweat losses
- Following exercise drink 450-675 mL for every 0.5 Kg of body weight lost or (16-24 oz for every pound)

A good indicator of hydration is urine color. When optimally hydrated urine should be a near clear pale yellow, darker colored urine indicates a state of dehydration. Proper hydration during exercise produces the following benefits:

- A less pronounced increase in heart rate
- A less pronounced increase in core body temperature
- Improvement in cardiac stroke volume & cardiac output
- Improvement in skin blood flow *(enabling better sweat rates & improved cooling)*
- Maintenance of better blood volume
- A reduction in net muscle glycogen usage *(improving endurance)*

Nutrition & Health

Glucose is a simple sugar that is the preferred energy source for the human body. It is a compound of many carbohydrates. Some carbohydrates (glucose) are required for the oxidation (burning) of fat & also help keep protein (muscle tissue) from being broken down. However too much glucose (carbs/sugar) causes an excessive insulin response that encourages the production of fat. **Glycemic index** is measure of how carbohydrates affect blood sugar levels. Low glycemic foods help maintain glucose (blood sugar) levels that in turn maintains insulin balance which helps to keep the body out of the "fat storing" state. Blood glucose reaches peak an hour after a meal & returns to normal 2 hours after that, therefore eating every 2-4 hours helps avoid mental & muscle fatigue. **Glycogen** is the storage form of glucose that is found in the liver & muscle tissues.

Dietary fiber is a carbohydrate that cannot be digested but aids in lowering fat & cholesterol absorption. Dietary fiber also improves blood sugar control. Since dietary fiber is non-digestible it is subtracted from the total carbohydrate amount of a given food. *If a food has 22 grams of total carbohydrates with 12 grams of dietary fiber then it has 10 grams of net carbs.*

Consuming polyunsaturated & monounsaturated "healthy fats" along with regular exercise has been shown to improve lipid profiles. Regular exercise also helps to reduce LDL cholesterol.

The human body is incapable of using protein for anabolic (tissue-building) purposes above the level of 1.5 grams per kilogram of body weight. Overconsumption of protein in excess of this amount is either burned as a source of energy or stored as fat. Excess protein also has to be excreted by the kidneys which can lead to increased metabolic waste and dehydration.

***Note** Personal Trainers can and **should** share general nonmedical nutrition information with their clients. See the **Nutrition Scope of Practice for ACE Fitness Professionals** in Appendix C starting on Page 726 of American Council on Exercise Personal Trainer Manual - Fifth Edition.*

The Female Athlete Triad is a health concern for active females. It involves three distinct conditions:
1) Disordered eating (poor nutritional behaviors such as anorexia & bulimia)
2) Amenorrhea (irregular or absent menstrual periods)
3) Osteoporosis (low bone mass & microarchitectural deterioration, which leads to weak bones & risk of fracture)

Anorexia Nervosa: An eating disorder characterized by low weight, fear of gaining weight, a strong desire to be thin & food restriction. Many people with the disorder still think they are overweight even though they are underweight.

Bulimia Nervosa: An eating disorder that involves binge eating followed by purging.

Binge eating disorder: Characterized by binge eating without subsequent purging episodes.

Domain III: Program Progression & Modifications

Monitor, evaluate, and modify programs designed to improve health, fitness, weight, body composition, and metabolism, and maintain client adherence

The Transtheoretical Model (TTM)

The TTM Model is composed of these four components: Stages of change, Processes of change, Self-efficacy, and Decisional balance.

Stages of change: Pre-contemplation, Contemplation, Preparation, Action, Maintenance
*Know how to determine what stage of change the client is in based on their responses during motivational interviewing.

Process of change involves using interventions specific to a client's current stage of change to help them transition to the next stage of change. This will help increase the success of the client adopting a new behavior.

Self-Efficacy: The belief in one's own capabilities to successfully engage in a physical-activity program along with one's ability for self-management, goal achievement & effectiveness.

Self-Efficacy is developed through the following six sources of information: Past performance experience, Vicarious experience, Verbal persuasion, Physiological state appraisals, Emotional state and mood appraisals, and Imaginal experiences.

Decisional Balance involves the perceived pros and cons one has about adopting and/or maintaining an exercise program. In the early stages of pre-contemplation & contemplation the perceived cons usually outnumber the pros. While people in the later stages of action & maintenance perceive more pros than cons.

SMART Goals: *Specific, Measurable, Attainable, Relevant, Time-Bound*

A **Process goal** is a goal a person achieves by doing something *(the process)*, such as completing a certain number of workouts each week. A **Product goal** is something that is achieved *(the product)* such as weight loss or an increase in strength. The following four mechanisms play a role in goal-related behavior change:

- Goals direct attention toward desired behaviors
- Goals lead to greater effort
- Goals extend the time & energy devoted to a desired behavior
- Goals increase the use of goal-relevant skills

The Health Belief Model (HBM)

The perceived threat of a potential health problem, susceptibility to potential health consequences & the belief that making suggested behavioral changes will result in a decreased risk of those consequences.

Example would be a sedentary person who has high blood pressure that decides to regularly exercise & eat better to decrease their blood pressure naturally. They must believe that making those behavioral changes will decrease the health risk associated with high blood pressure.

Behavior-Change Strategies

Operant Conditioning is the process by which behaviors are influenced by their consequences. **Positive reinforcement** increases the future occurrence of that behavior. **Extinction** occurs when the positive stimulus that once followed a behavior is removed decreasing reoccurrence of that behavior. **Negative reinforcement** can also increase the reoccurrence of an undesirable behavior if the client does not have accountability or consequences for that behavior *(showing up late, lack of effort, etc.)* Personal trainers should provide the appropriate amount of feedback, encouragement and consequences to help clients maintain desired behaviors.

Decision making involves the ability to control a situation and choose the appropriate course of action. Effective decision making skills give control back to the person involved and allows them to dictate the next steps to take. Personal trainers should continuously provide their client's with knowledge that empowers them to take ownership and be successful on their own.

Client-Trainer Relationship

There are four stages of the client-trainer relationship: Rapport Stage, Investigation Stage, Planning Stage, and Action Stage.

Rapport is defined as a relationship marked by mutual understanding and trust. This stage begins with the initial first impressions a client has and continues to develop through the use of good verbal and nonverbal communication. A personal trainer should possess excellent communication and teaching skills to create a climate of trust and respect with the client. Expressing ***empathy***, warmth and genuineness are three attributes to building a successful client-trainer relationship. People don't care how much you know until they know how much you care. Future teachings and valuable information that a personal trainer has to share will go unheard if they have not built this foundation of mutual understanding, trust and respect with their clients. *Positive first impressions are the foundation for the rapport-building process.*

The ***Investigation*** stage involves gathering information and demonstrating effective listening skills. Identifying client's readiness to change behavior; their current stage of behavioral change and personality style; collecting health and safety information; learning about lifestyle preferences, interest, and attitudes; understanding previous experiences; and conducting assessments. *A trainer should be able to identify the emotional needs behind the client's decision to start and exercise program, and work with the client to address those needs.*

The ***Planning*** stage consists of the following steps: Setting goals, generating and discussing alternatives, formulating a plan, evaluating the exercise program, and designing motivation and adherence strategies.

The ***Action*** stage is where the exercise program begins. Implementing all of the programming components and providing instruction, demonstration, and execution of the programs; implementing strategies to improve motivation and promote long-term adherence; providing feedback and evaluation; making necessary adjustments to programs; and monitoring the overall exercise experience and progressions towards goals.

Communication & Teaching Techniques

Listen: Active listening involves nodding, making eye contact & restating important information the client has stated. Be nonjudgmental & open minded. Give oral & nonverbal feedback to indicate attention & understanding. Make sure to receive affirmation from client on feedback given. Identify statements that indicate a teaching and/or learning opportunity.

Empathize: Match the client's emotions to show affective empathy. The ability to identify with their perspective shows an understanding that helps to develop trust & rapport. *"Seek first to understand, and then to be understood."* – Stephen Covey

Positive Affirmation: Positive words promote positive attitudes & positive outcomes. Positive reinforcement & encouragement help the client to build self-esteem & motivation for exercise.

Intrinsic Motivation: Participation in exercise to achieve internal outcomes such as enjoyment of exercise itself or the sense of accomplishment after the workout is completed. Intrinsic motivation for exercise is better for lifelong adherence to exercise.

Extrinsic Motivation: Participation in exercise to achieve external outcomes such as weight loss & appearance. Extrinsic motivation is good for short term SMALL goals. External motivation from trainer should inspire intrinsic motivation of the client.

Motivational Interviewing: Helps a client commit to changing unhealthy behavior by combining empathetic counseling & a direct approach to decisive change. Ask open-ended questions that require more than a "yes" or "no" answer. Encourage the client to talk about what needs to be changed & then help them find ways to elicit that behavior change. Personal trainers should empower their clients to take control, be independent and self-sufficient with their exercise program by teaching and helping them find enjoyment in the experience. Helping clients take ownership and control increases their intrinsic motivation. A personal trainer should not try to control or manipulate a client into acting a certain way as this will diminish the intrinsic motivation of the client.

Self-Esteem: Confidence in one's self-worth or abilities.

Self-Concept: Perceived worthiness, capabilities & skills of one's self based on inner belief & the responses of others.

Types of Learners

Visual: Someone who learns through seeing images & techniques. Visual learners must first see what they are expected to know.

Auditory: A person who learns best through listening. They depend on hearing & speaking as a main way of learning.

Kinesthetic: This learning style requires that you manipulate or touch material to learn. It is often combined with auditory or visual learning techniques producing multi-sensory learning.

"Tell, Show, Do" *Tell me and I'll forget, Show me and I may remember, Involve me and I'll understand.* Trainers should keep this proverb in mind when teaching exercises to clients. Using a combination of *"Tell, Show, Do"* is the best practice when teaching. Starting with a brief and simple explanation *"Tell"* along with demonstration *"Show"* followed by the client performing the exercise *"Do"*. The personal trainer should observe the client while they perform the exercise and prepare to provide helpful feedback.

Types of Feedback

Evaluative: A summary for the client of how well they have performed a given task.
e.g. "You maintained great form & control during that set."

Supportive: Encourage the client when they perform a task properly. This type of feedback is motivational for the client & helps them adhere to the exercise program.
e.g. "Great job on that last set! Way to finish strong!"

Descriptive: Specific information that helps the client understand what they need to do in order to improve.
e.g. "Make sure to keep your core tight & back straight during the deadlift to protect from injury."

*The type of feedback that provides information on progress can be referred to as **knowledge of results**.

Client Feedback

Seeking client feedback will help the personal trainer ensure client satisfaction & enjoyment of the program. Paying attention to both verbal & nonverbal feedback will assist the trainer in properly progressing and modifying the clients training program as needed. Scheduling periodic program evaluations & goal reviews will also ensure client expectations are met.

Adherence to Exercise

* It takes about 6 months of regular exercise to see lasting health benefits.
* 50% of people who begin an exercise program quit within 6 months.
* Involving clients in the planning stage of an exercise program by asking for their input and working together to design the program helps them take responsibility for the program and increases exercise adherence.
* An individual who perceives that the benefits of exercise outweigh the barriers to exercise is more likely to adhere to an exercise program.
* Helping clients achieve their own *self-regulation* for exercise is necessary to increase exercise adherence. Self-regulation strategies include planning exercise, setting exercise-related goals, self-monitoring exercise behavior & avoiding relapse.

Overcoming Barriers

Factors influencing exercise participation & adherence: Personal Attributes *(Demographic Variables, Health Status, Activity History, Psychological Traits, Knowledge, Attitudes, and Beliefs)* Environmental Factors *(Access to Facilities, Time, and Social Support)* Physical-Activity Factors *(Intensity and Injury)*

Personal Barriers: These can be internal or behavioral such as lack of time, motivation, knowledge, injury & extrinsic motivation. Discussing strategies for time management, sharing information about the benefits of exercise & setting challenging but attainable goals can help increase a client's self-efficacy to overcome personal barriers.

Social Barriers: These barriers arise from within the client's social network (close family & friends). Examples of social barriers include caregiving (such as child care), lack of social support & sociocultural barriers. Understanding what types of social support a client needs & teaching them how to obtain that support may help them achieve the support required to adhere to exercise. Social support has four types: *Emotional, Tangible, Informational & Appraisal*

Environmental Barriers: These are physical barriers that are often outside of an individual's control that prevent them from being active. Lack of access to exercise facilities, bad weather & safety concerns (absence of sidewalks or bike lanes, crime) are some examples. Providing clients with opportunities to be active outside of the gym, at their homes or within their daily lifestyles can help overcome lack of access.

Avoiding Relapse: Psychological factors & high-risk situations such as life events (births, deaths in the family), holidays, injuries, decreased social support & decreased motivation can impact continued adherence to exercise. These may cause a lapse (brief period of two or more weeks) or relapse (complete return to sedentary behavior) in exercise adherence. Discussing potential relapse situations before they occur with a client can prepare them to overcome & maintain their exercise routine. *Assertiveness* is an important characteristic for achieving success and avoiding relapse. The more assertive clients are with regard to their progress, concerns, accomplishments and struggles the more likely they are to achieve long term success. Continuing self-regulation, intrinsic motivation along with setting achievable goals will help a client's self-efficacy & prevention of relapse.

Special Populations Exercise Recommendations

Special populations include clients with the following health conditions or special needs:

- Coronary artery disease
- Hypertension
- Stroke
- Peripheral vascular disease
- Dyslipidemia
- Diabetes
- Metabolic syndrome
- Asthma
- Cancer
- Osteoporosis
- Arthritis
- Fibromyalgia
- Chronic fatigue syndrome
- Low-back pain
- Weight management
- Older adults
- Youth
- Pre- and postpartum

Clients with one or more of the above should engage in a low to moderate intensity **individualized** exercise program designed for their specific needs based on their current health status, physical condition, and other factors identified in the screening process. Personal trainers working with these types of clients should maintain close communication with the client's healthcare professionals and expand their own knowledge in the applicable areas.

Exercise should not continue if any of the following signs or symptoms are observed: *Angina (chest pain), dyspnea (shortness of breath), lightheadedness or dizziness, pallor (pale skin), or rapid heart rate above established targets.* Personal trainers should question their clients and be aware of such signs or symptoms before, during & immediately after each exercise session while also making sure clients can recognize these signs & symptoms as well. If systems are present & persist, the emergency medical system should be activated & the client's physician should be notified.

The following is a list of considerations when working with clients that have **Hypertension**:
*Avoid performing **isometric** exercises, inverted positions & the **Valsalva maneuver** because they can dramatically raise blood pressure and associated work of the heart.
*Many hypertensive clients will be on medication for the condition and some medications such as beta blockers & calcium channel blockers can alter the heart-rate response during exercise. Clients on these medications should be taught to use the RPE scale to monitor exercise intensity.
*Diuretic medications are also used to control blood pressure & special attention to hydration is needed for clients on these medications to avoid dehydration, especially in warm environments.

Dyslipidemia: Elevated levels of LDL & total cholesterol. Dyslipidemia is best managed and improved by combining exercise with dietary changes that reduce body fat & weight.

Stroke: A sudden and often severe attack due to blockage of blood flow or bleeding in the brain. The following are warning signs of a stroke that personal trainers should be aware of:
- Walk: Is the victim's balance off? (walking problems, dizziness, or loss of coordination)
- Talk: Is the victim's speech slurred or face droopy? (confusion, trouble speaking or understanding others)
- Reach: Is one side week or numb? (numbness or weakness of the face, arms or legs)
- See: Is the victim's vision all or partially lost? (trouble seeing in one or both eyes)
- Feel: Does the victim have a severe headache with no known cause?

Peripheral Vascular Disease (PVD): Clients with PVD may also have underlying **coronary artery disease (CAD)** and develop symptoms as walking distance, speed or intensity increases. If symptoms are present exercise should be discontinued until the client is evaluated by their physician.

Clients with PVD should avoid exercising in cold air or water to reduce the risk of vasoconstriction (narrowing of blood vessels).

Diabetes Control: The primary treatment goals for diabetes are to normalize glucose metabolism and prevent diabetes-associated complications and disease progression. Proper management of diabetes is required by the individual as well as their physicians, diabetes educators, dietitians, exercise specialist, etc. Personal trainers can provide assistance by motivating the client to participate in regular physical activity and provide necessary feedback to the team regarding progress and responses.

Clients with diabetes should check their blood sugar prior to exercise to ensure their blood glucose level is between 100 and 250 mgdL. If they are below 100 mgdL then they should consume a pre-exercise snack that is high in complex carbohydrates and low in fat. Extra calories may need to be consumed *(such as a sports drink)* during or after exercise to maintain blood sugar levels. If a person has a blood sugar level of 250 mgdL with the presence of ketones in their urine or 300 mgdL without ketones then exercise should not be performed until blood sugar is better controlled.

Proper footwear is essential for clients with diabetes or PVD to prevent constriction, ulcers or injury due to "peripheral neuropathy," which causes loss of sensation in the extremities.

Asthma: Most people with controlled asthma will benefit from regular exercise and can follow general population guidelines. Individuals with asthma should perform gradual & prolonged warm-up & cool-downs to lessen the response during higher-intensity exercise performed during the conditioning phase. Exercise conditioning can reduce the ventilatory requirement for various tasks making it easier for asthmatic individuals to perform daily activities and sports as well as reduce the severity of exercise-induced asthma (EIA) attacks.

Metabolic Syndrome (MetS) is a cluster of three or more of the following conditions:

- Elevated waist circumference *(≥40" for men & ≥35" for women)*
- Elevated triglycerides *(≥150 mg/dL)*
- Reduced HDL cholesterol *(<40 mg/dL for men & <50 mg/dL for women)*
- Elevated blood pressure *(≥130/85 mmHg)*
- Elevated fasting blood glucose *(≥100 mg/dL)*

The presence of MetS increases a person's risk for developing heart disease, type 2 diabetes, and stroke. The primary treatment objective for MetS is to reduce those risks through lifestyle interventions such as healthy eating, increased physical activity, weight loss, and tobacco cessation.

Cancer: The goal with exercise in treatment of cancer is to help improve one's overall quality of life thru cardiovascular conditioning, preventing musculoskeletal deterioration (atrophy), reducing symptoms such as nausea & fatigue, and improving the client's mental health. The training program should be individualized to fit each client's needs and should focus on aerobic activities, light strength training, and stretching while also including recreational activities.
***Note**: Adequate cardiorespiratory training will decrease the chance of relapse in breast cancer patients.*

Osteoporosis: Decreased bone mineral density (BMD) and deterioration in bone microarchitecture. This condition causes structural weakness and increases the risk of a fracture. Resistance training, especially higher intensity can increase BMD and strength reducing the risk of falls and fractures. When working with clients that have osteoporosis some activities may need to be modified or avoided to prevent further injury and falls. Clients with osteoporosis should obtain medical clearance from their physicians prior to beginning an exercise program.

Arthritis: Characterized as inflammation of a joint. Exercise programs for those with arthritis should be designed based on the functional status of the client. These programs should be designed in conjunction with the client's physician or physical therapist. The goals of the program are to improve cardiovascular fitness and lower CAD risk, increase muscular endurance and strength, and maintain or, when indicated, improve range of motion and flexibility around the affected joints.

Fibromyalgia: Characterized by long-lasting widespread pain and tenderness at specific pints on the body. Studies have shown that exercise can ease symptoms of fibromyalgia and prevent the development of other chronic conditions associated with physical inactivity. Aerobic exercise in particular can significantly reduce pain, depression, and anxiety frequently associated with fibromyalgia.

Chronic Fatigue Syndrome (CFS): Unexplained persistent fatigue that last more than six months resulting in substantial reduction in previous levels of activity. Moderate to vigorous intensity exercise is not recommended for people with CFS as it can exacerbate fatigue and other symptoms that could last for days or weeks making the condition worse. Lower intensity activity with appropriate rest has been shown to decrease stress, improve fatigue, functional capacity, and overall fitness.

Low-Back Pain (LBP): A training program for those with LBP should consist of cardiorespiratory training, resistance training, and basic core exercises. The presence of pain is an indication of improper technique and exercises that cause LBP should be avoided. Unsupported forward flexion, twisting at the waist with turned feet while carrying a load, lifting both legs together when in a prone or supine position, and rapid movements involving twisting, forward flexion, or hyperextension are examples of what to avoid.

Weight management: Caloric consumption and physical inactivity are directly related to obesity but are not the only causes. In many cases, obesity is caused by complex psychosocial issues that may require referral to a psychologist or professional counselor. Detailed medical, physical-activity, and dietary histories are necessary before a physician can begin to determine the cause of obesity in patients.

Older Adults: All older adults have experienced a loss of physical fitness with age, some more than others. Many also have one or more chronic conditions that vary in type and severity. The extent to which exercise can affect cardiovascular, endocrine, respiratory, and musculoskeletal systems in older adults is not fully understood.

Youth: Physical inactivity, poor dietary habits and other unhealthy behaviors established at a young age have a high probability of persisting into adulthood which increases the risk of premature death. Children & adolescents from ages 6-17 years old should participate in at least 60 minutes per day of moderate to vigorous intensity exercise. Children should participate in vigorous intensity, muscle & bone strengthening activities at least three days per week.

Pregnant Women: Should obtain physician clearance and guidelines for exercise before initiating an exercise program ensuring there are no health conditions present that would limit activity. Women who are pregnant should avoid exercises in the supine position after the first trimester.

Domain IV: Professional Conduct, Safety, & Risk Management

Fulfill responsibilities through ongoing education, collaboration, and awareness of professional standards and practices necessary to protect clients, stakeholders, and the personal trainer.

ACE Certified Personal Trainer Scope of Practice

Read & understand the ACE Certified Personal Trainers' scope of practice on Pages 8, 9 & 10 of *American Council on Exercise Personal Trainer Manual - Fifth Edition*.

Note Claims related to violations of scope of practice most frequently occur in the area of supplements. Unless a personal trainer is also a registered dietitian or a physician, he or she does not have the expertise or legal qualifications necessary to recommend supplements. See **Nutrition Scope of Practice for ACE Fitness Professionals in Appendix C starting on Page 726 of American Council on Exercise Personal Trainer Manual - Fifth Edition.*

An ACE Certified Personal Trainer (CPT) must **always** operate within their **scope of practice** & refer clients to other **allied healthcare professionals** when necessary. Refer to Physicians, physical therapist, registered dietitians, chiropractors, or any other healthcare specialist.

*Note these referrals can take place at any point during the trainer-client relationship. (During the initial screening, a training session or evaluations down the line)

Read & understand the **ACE Code of Ethics** in "Appendix A" starting on Page 710 of *American Council on Exercise Personal Trainer Manual - Fifth Edition*.

Business Plan

Personal trainers must make the important decision to either work for an employer, work as an independent contractor, or start their own training business as an entrepreneur. Working for an employer is a good option for personal trainers who are just starting out as they can learn about the industry without having to take the time and financial risks involved with operating a business on their own. Once they gain experience they can venture off as an independent contractor or start their own business.

Personal trainers should take some time conducting market research to ensure the target demographic *(prospective customers)* have the means and access to the trainers potential work environments. Developing a unique skillset that is tailored to the specific goals of this customer base will help the trainer build their "brand" of training.

A business plan should cover all of the following: *Executive summary, Business description, Marketing plan, Operational plan, Risk analysis, Decision-making criteria.*

A **Financial plan** should provide the specific details for how a business will generate cash flow and produce a profit. The personal trainer should be a specific as possible and consider all of the potential issues related to cash flow in the planning process. This will allow them to focus time on operation once the business is open.

Personal trainers should stay up to date on the standards of care and accepted business practices by reading publications and attending conference presentations that address legal issues.

Regular consultation with an attorney who is aware of the unique laws governing the trainer's city, state, and county will help to ensure that legal responsibilities are met and upheld. This will help to mitigate potential litigation and other legal concerns.

The following are the most popular times for clients to work with trainers:

- Morning 5AM – 9AM (before work)
- Afternoon 12PM – 2PM (lunch break)
- Evening 4PM – 8PM (after work)

Six basic business models

Sole Proprietorship: One person owns the business.
Partnership: Two or more people who form a business together.
*Any potential partnership can become contentious and should not be entered without considerable contemplation and legal advice.
Independent Contractor: Provides certain services for other individuals or businesses.
*Note the difference between an independent contractor who is paid per job or task on a short term basis and an employee who works for an employer and is compensated on a regular basis.
Corporation: A formal business entity subject to laws, regulations and the demands of stockholders. A corporation is a legal entity completely separate from its owners & managers.
S Corporation (Subchapter Corporation): Combines the advantages of sole proprietorship, partnership, and corporation business models. Suitable alternative for small businesses.
Limited Liability Company: Flexible for small & medium sized business and generally more advantages than partnerships or S corporations.

*Advantages and disadvantages of these various business structures can be found in Table 17-1 on Page 645 of American Council on Exercise Personal Trainer Manual - Fifth Edition. Consulting with an attorney that specializes in this area can reduce potential liability and mitigate potential tax payments.

Legal Documentation & Laws

Negligence: A failure to perform as a reasonable and prudent professional would perform under similar circumstances. A reasonable and prudent person is someone who adheres to the established standard of care.
*Slip-and-fall injuries, equipment issues, free weights, weight machines, cardiovascular machines & claims of sexual harassment are common areas of negligence seen in training settings. *The four elements that a plaintiff must prove in a negligence claim are duty, breach of duty, proximate cause, and damages.*

Contracts provide the best method to ensure that all aspects of a relationship are properly established. Whether a trainer works as an independent contractor or employee the basic tenets of contract law should be understood.

Waiver: Voluntary abandonment of a right to file suit; not always legally binding. It is recommended that personal trainers utilize their own waivers in addition to any waivers potentially signed by a client when they joined the fitness center or club where the trainer is employed. Investigation with an attorney prior to creating a waiver is recommended as each state has their own rules regarding waivers.

Agreement to participate is a signed document that indicates the client is aware of the inherent risks and potential injuries that can occur from participation in exercise.

Informed consent is a written statement signed by a client prior to testing that informs them of testing purposes, process, and all potential risks and discomforts.

__Note__: Waivers, informed consent, and agreement to participate are ways the personal trainer can make the client aware of inherent risks involved in participation and avoid or defend against potential negligence claims.

Tort Law: Body of law that regulates civil wrongdoing.

HIPAA (Health Insurance Portability & Accountability Act): Law that requires health care professionals to have strict policies regarding the safety and security of private records. Written permission from the client must be obtained prior to sharing confidential information with an outside party.

FERPA (Family Educational Rights and Privacy Act): Federal privacy law that gives parents certain protections with regard to their children's education records and some control over the disclosure of information from the records.

Risk Management Program

Risk management is a process whereby a service or program is delivered in a manner to fully conform to the most relevant standards of practice and that uses operational strategies to ensure day-to-day fulfillment, ensure optimum achievement of desired client outcomes, and minimize risk of harm to clients. Risk management protocol should consist of the following five steps: *Risk identification, Risk evaluation, Selection of an approach for managing each risk, Implementation, and Evaluation. *Additional information can be found on Page 669 of American Council on Exercise Personal Trainer Manual - Fifth Edition.*

The following forms should be kept & maintained to ensure business practices conform to the standards set by professional organizations:

1) Preactivity Screening Form (PAR-Q)
2) Health History Questionnaire
3) Physician's Statement & Medical Clearance Form
4) Fitness Assessment or Evaluation Form
5) Release, Waiver, or Informed Consent
6) Client Progress Notes
7) Incident Reports

***Note**: Using the above tools and forms will help identify high-risk individuals who need medical referral or require modifications to their exercise program. High-risk clients with cardiac disease are 10 times more likely to have a cardiovascular event during exercise than those who are apparently healthy.*

A business and/or personal trainer should carry **professional liability insurance** which transfers the risk to the insurance company in the event of an incident or claim by a client. The best insurance policies cover the cost of legal defense and any claims awarded. ACE recommends retaining at least 1 million in coverage. The following is a link for reputable insurance carriers who specialize in the fitness industry www.ACEfitness.org/insurancecenter/

Client confidentiality must also be kept & protected to prevent potential harm to a client's reputation & liability to the personal trainer or business. The personal trainer or business must obtain and store a signed release form before disclosing any personal information about a client. *This includes posting a client's results (before & after photos, etc...)*

Emergency Procedures

All organizations or personal trainers that operate independently must have an emergency action plan in place. The facility must also have an AED onsite. Personal trainers & staff who are responsible for working directly with clients must have current **CPR (Cardiopulmonary Resuscitation) & AED (Automated External Defibrillator)** certifications. Failure to abide by the emergency procedures can expose the trainer to legal liability. The federal government passed the Cardiac Arrest Survival Act in 2000 which protects the person who administers an AED during an emergency from liability. Many states also have Good Samaritan laws that offer liability protection to the person who administers the AED.

Injury Prevention Program

An area of Tort Law called *"premises liability"* regulates any incidents that result from conditions of the physical setting where training activities occur. Any training setting or premises must have a reasonably safe environment. Exercise equipment service plans along with routine inspections & maintenance of equipment should be performed in order to reduce the potential risk of injury. If an unsafe condition is noticed, the trainer should notify the facility's management and avoid that area until it has been addressed. Providing a safe environment along with the emergency action plan mentioned above will help to mitigate potential liability for incidents that may occur during a training session. *The number one claim against fitness facilities and professionals is for injuries related to falls on the training premises.*

When to call 9-1-1

It is appropriate to call emergency medical services (EMS) when there is a life-threatening situation or anything that requires immediate medical attention. The following situations where someone is seriously ill, is not breathing, has an open wound to the chest, or is bleeding profusely warrant contacting 9-1-1. *For additional situations that require contacting EMS see key concept on Page 608 of American Council on Exercise Personal Trainer Manual - Fifth Edition.*

Cardiac arrest is the cessation of heart function, when a person loses consciousness, has no pulse, and stops breathing. The following Chain of Survival *(four steps)* developed by the American Heart Association (AHA) can increase the likelihood of survival:

- Early access
- Early CPR
- Early defibrillation
- Early advanced care

Without treatment, the person's chance of survival decreases by 10% for every minute that passes. CPR should ideally begin within two minutes of the onset of cardiac arrest. EMS usually takes an average of 7-10 minutes to arrive once contacted so CPR should be performed by a bystander, friend, family member or stranger as it can more than double the chance of survival.

Common Medical Emergencies and Injuries

Dyspnea occurs when a person has difficult and labored breathing. In some situations dyspnea can come on suddenly and be very uncomfortable and even life-threatening. Trainers should be aware of the signs of respiratory distress including poor movement of the chest wall, flaring of the nostrils, straining of the neck muscles, poor air exchange from the mouth and nose, pale sweaty skin, and **Cyanosis** *(bluish color that develops around the lips, nose, fingernails, and inner lining of the eyes)*. To asses breathing in an unconscious person, a personal trainer should feel for air flow on their own cheek while looking for the chest to rise and fall while also listening for unusual snoring, gurgling, or high pitched sounds that may indicate a partial airway blockage. If the person is **apneic** *(not breathing)* no chest movement or sounds indicating air movement, the personal trainer should give breaths. If there is no pulse then CPR should be initiated.

Choking: A person who is chocking will have a partially or completely blocked airway. If the person cannot breathe, make sounds, or has a very quiet cough, or if a child cannot cry, the blockage is severe. The **Heimlich maneuver** should be performed. The rescuer should stand behind the victim with both arms wrapped around the victim's waist, make a fist with one hand, and put the thumb side just above the victim's belly button. The other hand should grab this fist and perform several upward thrust to compress the diaphragm and force the object out of the victim's airway. If the victim is very large or in the late stages of pregnancy, the rescuer can wrap their arms around the victim's breastbone instead of the abdomen. If the Heimlich maneuver does not work, the victim may become unconscious. If this occurs someone should call for help and CPR should be initiated.

Heart Attack: A heart attack is caused by an obstruction in a coronary vessel that prevents part of the heart muscle from getting adequate blood flow and oxygen. The warning signs and symptoms of a heart attack include **angina pectoris** *(chest pain / pressure)*, pain can also be felt in one or both arms *(usually the left arm)*, the neck, jaw, shoulder, or stomach, there can also be shortness of breath, nausea, a cold sweat, and lightheadedness. Most heart attack warning signs have a gradual onset that is not sudden and intense. Delay in treatment can be fatal. Personal trainers should be able to recognize signs of a heart attack as the person experiencing the symptoms may not realize what is happening or be in denial.

Heat Stress: There are various types of heat stress that can occur with exercise in hot and humid conditions such as heat edema, heat cramps or more serious conditions such as **heat exhaustion** *(profuse sweating, cold clammy skin, dizziness, weak rapid pulse)* and **heat stroke** *(hot dry skin, bright red skin color, strong rapid pulse)*. Clients should exercise during cooler times of the day such as morning or evening, take more frequent water breaks on very hot & humid days, and avoid exercise in extremely hot and humid conditions with a wet bulb global temperature (WBGT) above 82°F. *For additional information see Tables 16-2 & 16-3 on Pages 619 & 621 of American Council on Exercise Personal Trainer Manual - Fifth Edition.*

Cold Stress: Hypothermia and frostbite can occur when exposed to extreme cold climates or conditions. Proper preparation is necessary to avoid overexposure to the cold. Clothing should be layered to trap body heat and help maintain body temperature. Hats & gloves can also be used to prevent frostbite in exposed areas.

Contraindicated exercises: Movements or positions that are not recommended due to the potential injury risk associated. Examples include full squats, straight-leg sit ups, double leg raises, standing bent over toe touch, cervical & lumbar hyperextension, etc.

Concussion: A head injury with a loss of brain function, concussion causes a variety of physical, cognitive, and emotional symptoms, which may not be recognized as the initial signs can be subtle. Personal trainers should be aware of the following warning signs following a possible brain injury:

- Amnesia
- Confusion
- Memory loss
- Headache
- Drowsiness
- Loss of consciousness
- Impaired speech
- Tinnitus
- Unequal pupil size
- Nausea
- Vomiting
- Balance problems or dizziness
- Blurry or double vision
- Sensitivity to light or noise
- Any change in the individual's behavior, thinking, or physical function

Note: There are common misconceptions between loss of consciousness and concussions. A loss of consciousness does not always accompany a concussion and if a person does not lose consciousness it does not mean the concussion is minor. Trainers must understand that no concussion (brain injury) is ever minor.

Neck and Back Injuries: It is important that further damage is prevented if a neck injury is suspected. The victim should not be moved and head must be immobilized until EMS arrives.

Precautions and protection against bloodborne pathogens: Rescuers should wear gloves, use a protective barrier device when performing CPR, and wear eye protection and gown if there is potential for blood to splash on the rescuer. These precautions can help prevent the spread of bloodborne diseases such as hepatitis B and HIV when dealing with another person's blood or bodily fluids. Hand washing is the best way to prevent the spread of disease whether or not gloves were worn.

Musculoskeletal Injury Terms

Sprain: A stretching or tearing of ligaments.
Strain: A stretching or tearing of muscles or tendons.
Fractures: The breaking of a bone.
Patello-femoral pain syndrome: Pain in the front of the knee.
Low back pain: Pain in the lower back resulting from issues with the muscle and/or bones of the lower back.
Shin splints: Acute pain in the shin & lower leg cause by prolonged running, typically on hard surfaces.
Plantar fasciitis: Inflammation of the plantar fascia (thick band of tissue) that runs across the bottom of the foot & connects the heel bone to the toes.

Overuse Conditions

Tendonitis: Inflammation of a tendon and/or tendon-muscle attachment.
Fasciitis: Inflammation of the connective tissue called fascia.
Bursitis: Inflammation of a bursa, typically one in the knee, elbow or shoulder.
**Bursa* is a closed fluid-filled sac or cavity that reduces friction between tissues/joints in the body.

Upper-Extremity Injuries

Shoulder and Rotator Cuff Injuries: Specific guidelines should be obtained for what *"should"* and *"should not"* be done with a shoulder or rotator cuff injury during exercise. Modifications are often needed for overhead movements such as limiting range of motion (ROM) and adjusting shoulder position to help prevent impingement (pinching) and further injury. In general exercises with elbows bent are preferred over straight arm exercise as they create less torque on the healing tissues. **See Figures 15-3 & 15-4 on Pages 580 & 581 of American Council on Exercise Personal Trainer Manual - Fifth Edition.*

Elbow Tendinitis: High repetition exercises *(15-20 reps)* involving the elbow and wrist should be avoided for clients with elbow tendinitis. Exercises should begin with low weight and reps and gradually progress. Full elbow extension *(locking the elbow)* should be performed with caution as it can excessively load the muscles and cause further injury.

Carpal Tunnel Syndrome: Occurs when the median nerve becomes compressed at the wrist. Movements that involve full wrist flexion or extension to end-range positions can further compress the carpal tunnel exacerbating symptoms. Exercise should be performed in the mid-range of these motions for clients with carpal tunnel syndrome.

Lower-Extremity Injuries

Greater Trochanteric Bursitis: Inflammation of the trochanteric bursa, a part of the hip. This bursa is at the top, outer side of the femur. Avoiding side-lying positions that compress the lateral hip as well as higher-loading exercises such as squats and lunges will help prevent further injury until the condition heals. Aquatic exercises can be beneficial because the buoyancy of water can unload the hips and allow for gradual return to land-based exercises.

Iliotibial Band Syndrome (ITBS): A common overuse injury of the connective tissues located on the outer thigh and knee. Clients with ITBS should return slowly to activity with an exercise program that helps to regain flexibility and strength at the hip and lateral thigh. Early injury recognition along with using proper technique and equipment will aid in the healing process.

Patellofemoral Pain Syndrome (PFPS): Characterized as pain in the anterior *(front)* of the knee originating from the contact of the posterior surface of the patella with the femur. The causes of PFPS range from overuse, biomechanical, and muscle dysfunction. Restoring proper flexibility and strength is key with PFPS. Addressing tightness in the IT band complex, hamstrings, and calves through stretching and myofascial release *(foam rolling)* will help to restore balance across the knee joint. Exercises should focus on restoring proper strength throughout the hip, knee and ankle joints.

Infrapatellar Tendinitis: Inflammation of the patellar tendon connecting the kneecap *(patella)* to the shinbone. Often called "jumper's knee" this condition is caused by overuse and occurs frequently in sports and activities involving jumping aspects which put significant strain on the tendinous tissues in this area. The same protocol for restoring flexibility and strength in PFPS mentioned above should be used.

Shin Splints: A general term for any leg pain on the front or side of the lower leg in the region of the shin bone. Since overuse is the primary cause of shin splints rest and modified activity are best for symptom relief. Stretching and strengthening techniques for the lower leg *(foot, ankle, calves, and anterior leg muscles)* are also beneficial to restore any muscle imbalances in these areas.

Ankle Sprains: A person can usually resume exercise activity in 1-2 weeks after a Grade I sprain, 4-8 weeks after Grade II sprain, and 12-16 weeks after a Grade III sprain. Clients with ankle sprains will often lack stability with side-to-side and multidirectional motions. To prevent further injury exercise modification and progression should begin with straight-plane motions, then side-to-side, and lastly multidirectional motions.

Achilles Tendinitis: Inflammation of the Achilles tendon that connects the bones of your heel to your calf muscles. Controlled eccentric exercises for the calf complex can help relieve symptoms and improve strength.

Plantar Fasciitis: Often described as *"heel pain"* is caused by inflammation of the flat band of tissue *(ligament)* that connects the heel bone to the toes. Stretching of the plantar fascia, and calve muscles can help relieve symptoms. Self-myofascial release such as rolling the foot over a lacrosse ball, golf ball, or dumbbell may help to enhance range of motion (ROM) in the plantar fascia.

The Healing Process

Following an injury the body immediately starts the healing process using the following three phases:

Inflammatory phase: Immobilizes the injured area to begin the healing process. Blood flow is increased to bring in oxygen and nutrients to repair the damaged tissue. This phase can last for up to six days.

Fibroblastic/proliferation phase: The injured area fills with collagen and other cells which will eventually form a scar. This phase starts around day 3 and lasts until approximately until day 21. The wound can resist normal stresses within two to three weeks but strength continues to build for several months.

Maturation/remodeling phase: This final phase begins around day 21 by remodeling the scar, bone, or tissue that was injured into a more organized structure. This phase can last for up to two years.

Note*: Personal trainers must always by cautious with exercise progression for clients recovering from a musculoskeletal injury.*

The following treatment should be used immediately after musculoskeletal injuries such as sprains, strains, bruises & other soft-tissue injuries: **RICE**: *Rest, Ice, Compression, and Elevation*

A thorough medical history and assessment is recommended for clients who have a ***pre-existing injury***. The personal trainer should be able to determine if exercise is appropriate or if the client should be cleared by a medical professional prior to starting an exercise program. This will ensure the clients safety and provide appropriate guidelines to follow.

*The personal trainer must respect their defined **scope of practice** and refrain from diagnosing any injury themselves. If a client asks about an injury, the personal trainer should refer them to an appropriate healthcare provider and contact the provider to obtain guidelines and contraindications related to fitness training and the injured area.

*Modified exercise programs are appropriate for those with localized injuries. *(e.g. a client with an ankle sprain can still exercise the upper body and perform seated exercise that do not load the injured ankle.)*

Acronym & Abbreviation Meanings

ABCs: Airway, Breathing, Circulation, Severe bleeding (vital indicators in unresponsive person)

ACE IFT: ACE Integrated Fitness Training Model

ACL: Anterior Cruciate Ligament

ADL: Activities of Daily Living

AED: Automated External Defibrillator

ANS: Autonomic Nervous System

ASIS: Anterior Superior Iliac Spine

ATP: Adenosine Triphosphate (High energy compound required to do mechanical work)

BMD: Bone Mineral Density

BMI: Body Mass Index

BMR: Basal Metabolic Rate

BOS: Base of Support

CAD: Coronary Artery Disease

CFS: Chronic Fatigue Syndrome

CNS: Central Nervous System

COG: Center of Gravity

COM: Center of Mass

CPR: Cardiopulmonary Resuscitation

CRF: Cardiorespiratory Fitness

CVD: Cardiovascular Disease

DBP: Diastolic Blood Pressure

DDD: Degenerative Disc Disease

DOMS: Delayed Onset Muscle Soreness

Acronym & Abbreviation Meanings

DUP: Daily Undulating Periodization

EFI: Exercise-induced Feeling Inventory

EPOC: Excess Post Oxygen Consumption

FIRST: Frequency, Intensity, Repetitions, Sets and Type

FITT-VP: Frequency, Intensity, Time, Type, Volume & Progression

GTO: Golgi Tendon Organ

GXT: Graded Exercise Test

HIIT: High Intensity Interval Training

HRR: Heart Rate Reserve (Max HR - Resting HR)

IBW: Ideal Body Weight

LOG: Line of Gravity

LOS: Limits of Stability

MET: Metabolic Energy Equivalent (3.5 ml) an index of energy expenditure

MVC: Maximal Voluntary Contraction

OBLA: Onset of Blood Lactate Accumulation

PAR-Q: Physical Activity Readiness Questionnaire

PCr: Creatine Phosphate

PNF: Proprioceptive Neuromuscular Facilitation

PNS: Peripheral Nervous System

RCT: Respiratory Compensation Threshold

RDA: Recommended Daily Amount

RE-AIM: Reach, Efficacy, Adoption, Implementation & Maintenance

RER: Respiratory Exchange Ratio

Acronym & Abbreviation Meanings

RHR: *Resting Heart Rate*

RICE: *Rest, Ice, Compression & Elevation*

ROI: *Return on Investment*

ROM: *Range of Motion*

RMR: *Resting Metabolic Rate*

RPE: *Ratings of Perceived Exertion*

SAID: *Specific Adaptations to Imposed Demands*

SBP: *Systolic Blood Pressure*

SITS: *Supraspinatus, Infraspinatus, Teres minor, Subscapularis (Rotator Cuff Muscles)*

SMALL Goals: *Self-selected, Measurable, Action oriented, Linked to your life & Long term*

SMART Goals: *Specific, Measurable, Attainable, Relevant, Time-Bound*

SMR: *Self-Myofascial Release*

SOAP note: *Subjective, Objective, Assessment, Plan*

SSC: *Stretch Shortening Cycle*

SSRI: *Selective Serotonin Reuptake Inhibitors*

SWOT analysis: *Strengths, Weaknesses, Opportunities, Threats (Used for risk assessment)*

TIA: *Transient Ischemic Attack*

THR: *Target Heart Rate*

TTM: *The Transtheoretical Model*

TVA: *Transverse Abdominis*

WHR: *Waist to Hip Ratio*

Conversions

Fat = 9 calories per gram
Protein = 4 calories per gram
Carbohydrates = 4 calories per gram
Alcohol = 7 calories per gram
3500 kcal (calories) = 1 pound fat

1 Kg = 2.2 pounds (pounds ÷ 2.2 = Kg)
1 Inch = 2.54 cm (inches x 2.54 = cm)
1 Meter = 100 cm (cm ÷ 100 = Meters)
1 MET = 3.5 ml (VO$_2$ ÷ 3.5 = MET)

Formulas

Max Heart Rate (MHR): 220 – Age = MHR or 208 – (0.7 x Age) = MHR
e.g. 30 year old would have Max HR of 190 BPM | 220 – 30 = 190 BPM

Heart Rate Reserve (HRR): Max HR – Resting HR = HRR
e.g. 30 year old with resting HR of 60 BPM | 190 - 60 = 130 BPM

Target Heart Rate (THR) = HHR x % Intensity + Resting HR (Karoven Formula)
e.g. 30 year old mentioned above to train at 80% intensity | 130 x 0.80 + 60 = 164 BPM (THR)

Body Mass Index (BMI) = Weight (Kg) ÷ Height (m^2)
e.g. calculate the BMI of a man who is 6ft tall & weighs 180 pounds
180 ÷ 2.2 = 81.81 Kg | 6ft x 12 = 72 inches | 72 x 2.54 = 182.88 cm | 182.88 ÷ 100 = 1.83 m
| 1.83m^2 = 3.35 | 81.81 ÷ 3.35 = 24.42 BMI

Fat weight (FW) = Body weight (BW) x Body fat (BF) %
e.g. calculate based on 180 pound body weight & 20% body fat | 180 x 0.20 = 36 lbs of fat

Lean body weight (LBW) = Body weight (BW) – Fat weight (FW)
e.g. calculate based on information above | 180 – 36 = 144 lbs LBW

Desired Body Weight (DBW) = Lean body weight ÷ (100% - Desired body fat %)
e.g. calculate DBW if the person above wanted to be at 10% body fat | 144 ÷ 0.90 = 160 lbs

Waist to Hip Ratio (WHR) = Waist circumference ÷ Hip circumference
e.g. calculate based on an individual with 32-inch waist and 36-inch hip | 32 ÷ 36 = 0.89

1 Repetition Max (1RM) = Pounds lifted ÷ % of 1RM (See 1RM Table for % 1RM based on reps)
e.g. calculate based on 180 pounds lifted for 10 repetitions | 180 ÷ 0.75 = 240 pounds 1RM

Total calories from fat (FAT CAL) = Fat grams per serving x 9 kcal x # of servings per container

Percent of calories from fat (%FAT) = (Fat grams per serving x 9 kcal) ÷ Calories per serving

Calculation for daily caloric deficit to achieve desired weight loss in a set timeframe
Weekly caloric deficit = (Desired weight loss in pounds x 3500) ÷ # of weeks
Daily caloric deficit = Weekly caloric deficit ÷ 7

Practice Questions

1) John is a 53 year old former smoker who quit 8 months ago. His mother had a myocardial infraction at age 66. He has a fasting glucose of 100 g & regular blood pressure measurements of 140/95. How many risk factors does John have?

    A. 3
    B. 5
    C. 4
    D. 2

2) Using the information above what risk category would John fall under?

    A. Low
    B. Moderate
    C. High
    D. None of the Above

3) Which of the following movements does an overhead press exercise BEST mimic?

    A. Picking up a child
    B. Opening a door
    C. Picking an object up off the ground
    D. Putting a box on a high shelf

4) During load training it is recommended to increase the resistance by _____ once the end range repetitions are achieved in order to provide progressive overload and facilitate further strength development.

    A. 3%
    B. 5%
    C. 7%
    D. 10%

5) Which of the following musculoskeletal injuries describes a sprain?

   A. A stretching or tearing of muscles or tendons.
   B. Pain in the front of the knee.
   C. A stretching or tearing of ligaments.
   D. Inflammation of a tendon and/or tendon-muscle attachment.

6) What is the recommended minimum weekly amount of exercise for the general population?

   A. 300 Minutes
   B. 200 Minutes
   C. 150 Minutes
   D. 250 Minutes

7) "Only the muscles that are trained will adapt and change in response." BEST describes which of the following training principles?

   A. Overload
   B. Specificity
   C. Reversibility
   D. Periodization

8) Daniel is 6ft tall & weighs 180 pounds, what is his BMI calculation?

   A. 23.45
   B. 22.42
   C. 25.45
   D. 24.42

9) BMI cannot determine actual body composition, which means it can unfairly categorize which of the following types of individual?

   A. A person with a lot of body fat.
   B. An ectomorph with little muscle and body fat
   C. A person with a lot of muscle mass.
   D. None of the above.

10) Marie wants to lose 12 pounds by her wedding day which is 15 weeks away. Which of the following daily caloric deficits would be MOST effective to safely achieve her goal?

    A. 200 kcals caloric deficit combined with 200 kcals burned thru activity per day
    B. 500 kcals caloric deficit combined with 200 kcals burned thru activity per day
    C. 300 kcals caloric deficit combined with 300 kcals burned thru activity per day
    D. 200 kcals caloric deficit combined with 100 kcals burned thru activity per day

11) Joe is currently 200 pounds with a body fat percentage of 20%. He would like to reduce his body fat percentage to 14%. What would Joe's body weight be at the reduced body fat percentage?

    A. 181 pounds
    B. 176 pounds
    C. 190 pounds
    D. 186 pounds

12) There are 24 individual vertebrae in the spine. How many vertebrae make up the lumbar portion of the spine?

    A. 12
    B. 7
    C. 5
    D. 9

13) Mike recently had a physical check-up that was required by his employer. The physician recommended that Mike quit smoking and begin an exercise program to reduce his high cholesterol and high blood pressure. His employer paid for exercise sessions at the gym near their office. Mike expresses to the personal trainer that he is only there so he will not lose his job. Using the Transtheoretical Model what stage of change is Mike in?

    A. Contemplation
    B. Action
    C. Preparation
    D. Pre-contemplation

14) Which of the following describes proper position during the bend and lift screen?

   A. Tibia and torso are parallel to each other in the lowered position.
   B. Knees are lined up over the ankles in the lowered position.
   C. Quadricepses are parallel to the floor in the lowered position.
   D. None of the above

15) When a client is learning a new skill or exercise which stage of learning requires the MOST feedback from personal trainer?

   A. Cognitive
   B. Associative
   C. Autonomous
   D. Assertive

16) A personal trainer demonstrates proper exercise technique for the deadlift to a client while verbally describing the necessary movement pattern. After the client performs the exercise they ask the personal trainer to describe it again. What type of learner BEST describes this client?

   A. Visual
   B. Kinesthetic
   C. Evaluative
   D. Auditory

17) A client has recently missed multiple workout sessions. They have just started a new job that is further away from the gym and finding time to exercise has been difficult. They express frustration to their personal trainer. What is the MOST appropriate response the personal trainer can give?

   A. "You should prioritize your life and make time for exercise without excuses."
   B. "I understand your frustration; lapses are a normal part of the process. Let's create an exercise plan that better fits your new schedule."
   C. "Consistency is key to achieving your goals; you must make time for exercise in order to achieve them."
   D. "It's OK, let's just try to exercise more during your free time."

18) When exercising in a hot outside environment a client shows the following symptoms: High body temperature, dry red skin, rapid strong pulse. Which of the following conditions are they MOST likely experiencing?

    A. Heat stroke
    B. Heat edema
    C. Heat exhaustion
    D. Heat cramps

19) What is the recommended fluid intake amount post exercise?

    A. 17-20 ounces for every pound of weight lost
    B. 7-10 ounces for every pound of weight lost
    C. 16-24 ounces for every pound of weight lost
    D. 10-20 ounces for every pound of weight lost

20) A regular client has recently changed to a caloric restricted diet that does not include consuming animal protein. Although they have reached their goal weight they explain to their personal trainer that they feel weak and fatigued during workouts and ask them for advice. Which of the following responses should the personal trainer give?

    A. "You should supplement your diet with a complete protein such as whey protein powder to eliminate the fatigue you are feeling."
    B. "I know a great natural supplement company that has products to help increase energy. I will get you their information after our session."
    C. "You should take vitamin B12 to increase your energy levels."
    D. "I know a great dietician who can give you advice. I will get you their contact information after our session."

21) A client notes on a Health-history questionnaire that they are currently taking beta blocker medication for hypertension (high blood pressure). Which of the following methods of estimating exercise intensity should be used with this type of client?

    A. Target Heart Rate (THR) using the Karoven Formula
    B. Metabolic Energy Equivalents (MET)
    C. Ratings of Perceived Exertion (RPE)
    D. Target VO_2 using percentage of their VO_2 Max

22) The majority of people's communication is obtained by which of the following means?

   A. Verbal
   B. Nonverbal
   C. Listening
   D. Description

23) What is the recommended amount of time for the Warm-up period prior to exercise?

   A. At least 10 – 20 minutes
   B. At least 5 – 20 minutes
   C. At least 10 – 15 minutes
   D. At least 5 – 10 minutes

24) Tim is able to bench press 180 pounds for 10 repetitions. What is his predicted One Repetition Max (1RM) weight?

   A. 250 pounds
   B. 240 pounds
   C. 230 pounds
   D. 260 pounds

25) Which of the following exercise strategies is MOST effective for increasing power?

   A. Controlled slow repetitions with moderate resistance
   B. High velocity low repetitions with moderate resistance
   C. Heavy resistance with slow repetitions
   D. Low velocity high repetitions with light resistance

26) A personal trainer notices that one of the pedals on an elliptical machine has a screw missing and is unstable. What is the appropriate procedure to follow in this situation?

   A. Notify the facility's management and unplug the machine.
   B. Put a note on the machine to let people know it is defective.
   C. Notify the facility's management and block off that area until it has been addressed.
   D. Notify the other members in the gym so they don't use the machine.

27) Which of the following exercises would BEST target the pectoralis major muscles?

    A. Pull-ups
    B. Overhead press
    C. Body weight push ups
    D. Bench dips

28) The movement of the overhead shoulder press takes place in which plane of motion?

    A. Frontal
    B. Sagittal
    C. Transverse
    D. Horizontal

29) What is the optimal spotting position for the personal trainer when their client is performing an overhead dumbbell press?

    A. Behind the client with hands placed on or near their elbows
    B. In front of the client with hands placed on the weight.
    C. Behind the client with hands placed on or near their wrist below the weight.
    D. Behind the client with hands placed on the weight.

30) Which of the following sources of information would have the MOST influence on a client's self-efficacy who has just started an exercise program to lose weight?

    A. Another client's success story of losing weight.
    B. Their own past performance experience with exercise.
    C. Encouragement from their personal trainer.
    D. Self-appraisal of current fitness level.

31) What joint actions occur during the concentric portion of a deadlift?

    A. Knee extension, Hip flexion
    B. Knee flexion, Hip flexion
    C. Knee extension, Hip extension
    D. Knee flexion, Hip extension

32) Which of the following make up the hamstring muscle complex?

   A. Rectus femoris, Vastus lateralis, Vastus intermedius, Vastus medialis
   B. Biceps femoris (long & short heads), Semitendinosus, Semimembranosus
   C. Supraspinatus, Infraspinatus, Teres minor, Subscapularis
   D. Rectus abdominis, Gastrocnemius, Soleus, Calcaneus

33) If a person stands with ankle pronation, their knees will be _____?

   A. Internally rotated
   B. Neutral to the line of gravity
   C. Externally rotated
   D. Supinated

34) A client states that they have been experiencing neck and jaw pain that radiates to their left arm. What should the personal trainer do in this situation?

   A. Do some neck stretches at the end of their session to relieve tension in that area.
   B. Refer them to a physical therapist that can help alleviate the pain.
   C. Explain to them the implications of a possible heart attack and refer them to their physician for treatment and clearance to resume exercise.
   D. Recommend they take a few days off from exercising and take Advil for the pain.

35) During a static posture assessment a trainer notices the client stands with internally rotated shoulders and a rounded (slouched) back. What BEST describes this postural deviation?

   A. Lordosis
   B. Scoliosis
   C. Kyphosis
   D. Flat Back

36) A person with Lordosis would likely have which of the following muscle imbalances?

   A. Tight hip flexors and erector spinae, Weak abdominals and hip extensors
   B. Weak hip flexors and erector spinae, Tight abdominals and hip extensors
   C. Tight hip flexors and abdominals, Weak erector spinae and hip extensors
   D. Weak hip flexors and abdominals, Tight erector spinae and hip extensors

37) What form must be obtained from a client prior to performing assessments?

   A. Waiver
   B. Informed consent _(circled)_
   C. Client-trainer agreement
   D. Contract

38) Which of the following would be a contraindicated exercise for a client who has osteoporosis?

   A. Leg press at high-intensity (8-RM) _(circled)_
   B. Using an elliptical at moderate intensity
   C. Double leg V-ups
   D. Planks

39) Exercising for the enjoyment & long term health benefits describes which type of motivation?

   A. Social
   B. Extrinsic
   C. Environmental
   D. Intrinsic _(circled)_

40) Muscles that act primarily as stabilizers generally contain greater concentrations of which type of muscle fibers?

   A. Type I (slow-twitch) _(circled)_
   B. Type II (fast-twitch)
   C. Type IIx (intermediate)
   D. Sarcomeres

41) What muscle acts as a stabilizer during the push up?

   A. Latissimus dorsi
   B. Triceps
   C. Rectus abdominis _(circled)_
   D. Pectoralis major

42) When should a client's heart rate be checked during a cycle ergometer test?

   A. One minute after the test has been completed.
   B. One minute before & one minute after the test has been completed.
   C. Continually minute by minute during the test.
   D. Immediately after the test has been completed.

43) Which of the following should a personal trainer be aware of when working with a client who is on diuretics to maintain their high blood pressure?

   A. Dehydration
   B. Dyslipidemia
   C. Sinus bradycardia
   D. Claudication

44) Which blood pressure measurement is likely to decrease slightly or remain unchanged during exercise?

   A. Systolic blood pressure
   B. Diastolic blood pressure
   C. Resting blood pressure
   D. None of the above

45) What muscle fiber type is best suited for Olympic style lifters?

   A. Type IIx (intermediate)
   B. Type I (slow twitch)
   C. Type II (fast twitch)
   D. None of the above

46) Jane is a 35 year old with a resting heart rate of 50 BPM. What would her target heart rate be if she is looking to train at 80% intensity of her heart rate reserve (HRR)?

   A. 148 BPM
   B. 153 BPM
   C. 158 BPM
   D. 151 BPM

47) What is the smallest contractile unit of a muscle fiber that is responsible for the striated appearance of muscle tissue?

   A. Muscle spindle
   B. Sarcomere ✓
   C. Myosin (thick filament)
   D. Actin (thin filament)

48) Restoring proper muscle length-tension relationships are essential to good posture and functional movement patterns. What would be the appropriate action to correct postural kyphosis in a client?

   A. Stretch the upper back (trapezius) and strengthen the chest (pectoralis muscles)
   B. Strengthen the hip flexors and stretch the hip extensors
   C. Strengthen the upper back (trapezius) and stretch the chest (pectoralis muscles) ✓
   D. Stretch the hip flexors and strengthen the hip extensors

49) Which of the following describes Absolute Contraindication?

   A. The benefits of exercise outweigh the risk. Exercise testing can be done only after careful evaluation of the risk/benefit ratio.
   B. The risks of exercise testing outweigh the potential benefit. Client should not participate in exercise testing until conditions are stabilized or treated. ✓
   C. The risk/benefit of exercise testing is even. Exercise testing can be done only after careful evaluation of the risk/benefit ratio.
   D. None of the above

50) A personal trainer notices a person lying motionless on the floor in the locker room of their fitness facility. What is the FIRST thing the personal trainer should do in this situation?

   A. Call or tell someone to call for help.
   B. Immediately begin CPR and have someone prep the AED.
   C. Check their vital indicators ABC: *Airway, Breathing, Circulation* ✓
   D. None of the above.

Practice Question Answers

1) **A** / John has three risk factors for his age, fasting glucose of 100 & regular blood pressure measurements of 145/90.

2) **B** / John falls in the moderate risk category based on risk classification chart *(Figure 6-3 on Page 121 of American Council on Exercise Personal Trainer Manual - Fifth Edition)*

3) **D** / Putting a box on a high shelf.

4) **B** / 5% is the recommended increase when adding resistance.

5) **C** / A stretching or tearing of ligaments.

6) **C** / 150 minutes is the minimum weekly amount of exercise recommended.

7) **B** / Specificity

8) **D** / 24.42 | Body Mass Index (BMI) = Weight in Kg ÷ Height in m^2 (meters squared) | 180 ÷ 2.2 = 81.81 Kg | 6ft x 12 = 72 inches | 72 x 2.54 = 182.88 (1 inch = 2.54 cm) | 182.88 ÷ 100 = 1.83 (1 Meter = 100 cm) | 1.83^2 = 3.35 | 81.81 ÷ 3.35 = 24.42 BMI

9) **C** / A person with a lot of muscle mass.

10) **A** / 200 kcals caloric deficit combined with 200 kcals burned thru activity per day
15 weeks x 7 days a week = 105 days total | 12 pounds x 3500 *(calories per pound of fat)* = 42,000 calories to burn | 42,000 ÷ 105 = 400 calories per day deficit is required to lose 12 pounds in 15 weeks.

11) **D** / 186 pounds | Desired Body Weight = Lean body weight ÷ (100% - Desired body fat %) | 200 x 0.20 = 40 pounds of fat | 200 – 40 = 160 pounds of LBW | 160 ÷ (1.00 – 0.14) | 160 ÷ 0.86 = 186 pounds

12) **C** / 5 vertebrae make up the lumbar portion of the spine.

13) **D** / Pre-contemplation

14) **A** / Tibia and torso are parallel to each other in the lowered position.

15) **B** / Associative

16) **D** / Auditory

17) **B** / "I understand your frustration; lapses are a normal part of the process. Let's create an exercise plan that better fits your new schedule."

18) **A** / Heat stroke

19) **C** / 16-24 ounces for every pound of weight lost.

20) **D** / "I know a great dietician who can give you advice. I will get you their contact information after our session."

21) **C** / Ratings of Perceived Exertion (RPE)

22) **B** / Nonverbal

23) **D** / At least 5 – 10 minutes

24) **B** / 240 pounds | 180 ÷ 0.75 = 240lbs 1RM | See 1RM Table for % 1RM based on reps

25) **B** / High velocity low repetitions with moderate resistance.

26) **C** / Notify the facility's management and block off that area until it has been addressed.

27) **C** / Body weight push ups

28) **A** / Frontal

29) **C** / Behind the client with hands placed on or near their wrist below the weight.

30) **B** / Their own past performance experience with exercise.

31) **C** / Knee extension, Hip extension

32) **B** / Biceps femoris (long & short heads), Semitendinosus, Semimembranosus

33) **A** / Internally rotated

34) **C** / Explain to them the implications of a possible heart attack and refer them to their physician for treatment and clearance to resume exercise.

35) **C** / Kyphosis

36) **A** / Tight hip flexors and erector spinae, Weak abdominals and hip extensors

37) **B** / Informed consent

38) **C** / Double leg V-ups

39) **D** / Intrinsic motivation comes from within *(internal)* not external sources.

40) **A** / Type I (slow-twitch/endurance) muscle fibers are better suited for stabilizer muscles

41) **C** / Rectus abdominis

42) **C** / Continually minute by minute during the test.

43) **A** / Dehydration

44) **B** / Diastolic blood pressure

45) **C** / Type II (fast twitch) muscles fibers are better suited for explosive Olympic style lifts

46) **C** / 158 BPM | Target Heart Rate = Max HR - Resting HR x % of Intensity + Resting HR
220-35 = 185 Max Heart Rate | 185-50 x 0.80 + 50 = 158 BPM

47) **B** / Sarcomere

48) **C** / Strengthen the upper back (trapezius) and stretch the chest (pectoralis muscles)

49) **B** / The risks of exercise testing outweigh the potential benefit. Client should not participate in exercise testing until conditions are stabilized or treated.

50) **C** / Check their vital indicators ABC: *Airway, Breathing, Circulation.*

Resources & Helpful Links

The following links share additional insights that we found helpful when preparing for the ACE exam.

ACE Exam Content Outline
http://www.acefitness.org/fitness-certifications/pdfs/CPT-Exam-Content-Outline.pdf

ACE Certification Handbook
https://www.acefitness.org/fitness-certifications/pdfs/Certification-Exam-Candidate-Handbook.pdf

ACE Code of Ethics
http://www.acefitness.org/fitness-certifications/certified-code.aspx

ACE Study Center (Facebook)
https://www.facebook.com/ACEfitnessStudyCenter

ACE Exam Prep Blog
http://www.acefitness.org/blogs/2/exam-preparation-blog/

ACE Tools & Calculators
http://www.acefitness.org/acefit/tools-and-calculators/

ACE Personal Trainer Resources
https://www.acefitness.org/myace/login.aspx?returnUrl=%2fptresources%2fdefault.aspx

Personal Trainer Exam Prep (Facebook)
https://www.facebook.com/CPTPrep

Risk Factor Chart / Risk Stratification
http://www.acefitness.org/pdfs/ACSM-CAD-Risk-Factor-Chart.pdf

Test Taking Strategies
https://www.acefitness.org/blog/5305/set-yourself-up-for-success-with-these-test-taking

Nutrition Scope of Practice for ACE Fitness Professionals
https://www.acefitness.org/certifiednews/images/article/pdfs/NutritionScopeOfPractice.pdf

Thank You!

We want to thank you for choosing this study guide to help prepare for the ACE Exam. It is truly gratifying to share some insight & help you along your journey as a personal trainer. If you found value in the content provided you can follow the link below to leave a review expressing your thoughts.

http://www.amazon.com/gp/product-reviews/B01LCBXKDY

~ CPT Exam Prep Team

For additional insights or to leave feedback visit our Facebook page below.
https://www.facebook.com/CPTPrep

Your feedback is welcomed and appreciated!

References

1) American Council on Exercise Personal Trainer Manual (Fifth Edition).

Made in the USA
Lexington, KY
04 December 2016